Waste & Recycling Issues

Editor: Tracy Biram

Volume 385

independence
educational publishers

First published by Independence Educational Publishers

The Studio, High Green

Great Shelford

Cambridge CB22 5EG

England

© Independence 2021

Copyright

Photocopy licence

ISBN-13: 978 1 86168 843 9

Printed in Great Britain

Zenith Print Group

Contents

Introduction

Waste & Recycling Issues is Volume 385 in the issues series. The aim of the series is to offer current, diverse information about important issues in our world, from a UK perspective.

ABOUT WASTE & RECYCLING ISSUES

Recent research suggests that there will be more plastic in the ocean than fish by 2050. With the global population increasing, what is the solution to our waste problem? This book explores the plastic problem, and how to overcome it, as well as the importance of recycling.

We then also look at ways we can make positive changes for the environment and our lives, preserving the world for future generations.

OUR SOURCES

Titles in the **issues** series are designed to function as educational resource books, providing a balanced overview of a specific subject.

The information in our books is comprised of facts, articles and opinions from many different sources, including:

♦ Newspaper reports and opinion pieces

♦ Website factsheets

♦ Magazine and journal articles

♦ Statistics and surveys

♦ Government reports

♦ Literature from special interest groups.

A NOTE ON CRITICAL EVALUATION

Because the information reprinted here is from a number of different sources, readers should bear in mind the origin of the text and whether the source is likely to have a particular bias when presenting information (or when conducting their research). It is hoped that, as you read about the many aspects of the issues explored in this book, you will critically evaluate the information presented.

It is important that you decide whether you are being presented with facts or opinions. Does the writer give a biased or unbiased report? If an opinion is being expressed, do you agree with the writer? Is there potential bias to the 'facts' or statistics behind an article?

ASSIGNMENTS

In the back of this book, you will find a selection of assignments designed to help you engage with the articles you have been reading and to explore your own opinions. Some tasks will take longer than others and there is a mixture of design, writing and research-based activities that you can complete alone or in a group.

FURTHER RESEARCH

At the end of each article we have listed its source and a website that you can visit if you would like to conduct your own research. Please remember to critically evaluate any sources that you consult and consider whether the information you are viewing is accurate and unbiased.

Useful Websites

www.cariki.co.uk

www.gov.uk

www.greenecofriend.co.uk

www.greenpeace.org.uk

www.inews.co.uk

www.keepbritaintidy.org

www.loveMONEY.com

www.preventedoceanplastic.com

www.RecyclingBins.co.uk

www.telegraph.co.uk

www.thebalancesmb.com

www.theconversation.com

www.theecologist.org

www.thefirstmile.co.uk

www.theguardian.com

www.unisanuk.com

www.wearencs.com

www.wwf.org.uk

Five ways to reduce your household waste – and stop it being shipped to poorer countries

An article from The Conversation.

THE CONVERSATION

By Sankar Sivarajah, Head of School of Management and Professor of Technology Management and Circular Economy, University of Bradford

The UK is the largest plastic waste producer in Europe and one of the biggest producers of plastic waste in the world, second only to the US. The UK produces 99kg of plastic waste per person per year. And it exports about two-thirds of this waste to poorer countries such as Malaysia, Pakistan and Vietnam.

Shipping unsorted plastic waste from the European Union to non-OECD countries was banned by the EU from January this year. But the UK continues to export plastic waste to developing countries as part of new post-Brexit regulations.

Most of the plastic waste is sold to these countries as the UK currently does not have the means and capacity to process it at home. But these countries also lack the infrastructure and capacity to recycle imported waste. And waste that can't be recycled often ends up dumped in landfill or waterways or even burned – releasing toxic fumes into the environment. Indeed, much of the waste sent to these countries is unsorted and dirty plastics which can hardly be recycled anyway.

This trade of waste and the shifting of one country's problem onto another simply cannot continue. Our behaviour as consumers is central to tackling this huge amount of plastic waste – along with the 26 million tonnes of general household waste produced yearly in the UK. We therefore all need to start taking responsible actions and be held accountable for the waste we generate. Of course, changing behaviour is not easy or straightforward.

Cultivating change

In its latest report, the Climate Change Committee, which advises the UK Government on the path to achieving net-zero carbon, emphasises that change in consumer behaviour is one of the major ways to speed up decarbonisation. But this is not something that can simply be forced on people. As my research shows, people need to support any changes and have a willingness to take up new habits aligned with the zero-waste economy.

The good news is that the COVID-19 crisis has already shown that people are open to changing their consumption habits. Many have started to buy locally, are more interested in buying clothes made out of recycled materials, and aim to consume less meat.

For things to really change, we need an all-embracing approach that engages everyone and intervenes early on in how products are designed and consumed to solve the waste crisis. But there are small things that each one of us can do to prevent and produce less waste. Many of these solutions are based on principles from the circular economy – a concept that promotes the elimination of waste and continual use of products and materials.

Here are some affordable and practical tips:

Use less - stop and reflect on your wasteful consumption practices and simply use less (as many have during lockdown). Rethink your lifestyle and only use what you need for your daily living; not everything may be essential.

Buy local - in the early stages of the pandemic, with flights grounded and entry in and out of countries proving problematic, food shortages were abundant. Buying local proved to be the alternative. Buying local is not only better for the environment but it also helps to support your local economy and local producers.

Be resourceful - try your best to reuse, repair or upcycle before you decide to throw away things you think no longer work. Be creative in how you might repurpose products and materials. It may simply be giving a new lease of life to your old furniture with a touch of non-toxic paint instead of getting new pieces.

Think beyond recycling – recycling is good, but we consume more than we recycle. So avoid buying goods that you cannot recycle. This will push businesses to better design products and ultimately, design out wasteful materials.

Rethink ownership - there is a rise in new businesses adopting 'rental', 'pay per use' and 'on-demand' models for products ranging from clothes to furniture. So where possible do not buy things you use only occasionally; instead pay for access to these things when you need them.

Above all, it's important to remember that even very little change to our consumption habits takes us a step closer to reducing the UK's 26 million tonnes of household waste. Achieve that and it will ultimately put us on track for a more sustainable post-pandemic world.

15 February 2021

The world's most wasteful rich countries revealed

What a load of rubbish.

According to the World Bank's waste report, which calculates the amount of municipal solid waste (MSW) generated by each country, the US Virgin Islands is the planet's most wasteful country. But that's only part of the story as recycling rates are not available for all countries, such as the Virgin Islands or New Zealand. We reviewed the tonnes of waste generated per person after recycling, and found a very different story of the 30 richest yet most wasteful countries...

30. Spain: 0.36 tonnes per person

In 2017, the European Union identified almost 300 illegal landfill sites in Spain. So while it might only be the 30th most wasteful rich country on this list, Spain (the world's 49th richest country, according to the CIA World Factbook) is still one of the 14 countries the EU warns is at risk of missing the bloc's 2020 50% recycling target. Spain recycles 17% but has 20 million tonnes of MSW to deal with each year – 16.7 million after recycling, or 0.36 tonnes per person.

29. Portugal: 0.38 tonnes

Portugal has 4.7 million tonnes of waste to deal with annually and, although it has underground recycling systems, only 16% of waste is recycled, well below European averages. It is another country on the EU's hit list, along with Malta, Greece and Cyprus, with capital Lisbon's waste piles growing 10% in the last three years, largely due to tourism. The world's 67th richest country will ban restaurants and bars from offering single-use plastic containers next year.

Joint 26. France: 0.39 tonnes

France, one of the biggest contributors to the EU, is a surprising entry on this list. Its nearly 67 million people produce 33 million tonnes of waste a year and only recycle 22%. *The Economist* Intelligence Unit says it is the top country in the world for food sustainability, with law in the 41st richest country forbidding food waste by supermarkets – but less than 25% of plastic packaging is recycled and the country will only be banning plastic bags from next year.

Joint 26. Ireland: 0.39 tonnes

Ireland, the fifth European country to sit at the bottom of this list, is a country in crisis after China closed its doors to overseas recycling last year. The world's 10th richest country produces 2.7 million tonnes of waste annually and recycles a third, leaving 1.8 million tonnes (0.39 tonnes per person) to incinerate or dump. Eurostat figures show that Ireland is the biggest producer of plastic waste – nearly all of which used to be taken by China.

Joint 26. Netherlands: 0.39 tonnes

The Netherlands has 8.9 million tonnes of waste to manage each year, recycling a quarter. The world's 23rd richest country is taking some novel approaches to waste disposal, from a bike path made of recycled plastic to a supermarket selling chutneys, soaps and booze made from wonky or blemished fruit and vegetables. The Dutch government aims to halve the amount of food its people throw away to meet the EU's stringent waste goals by 2030.

25. Russian Federation: 0.4 tonnes

Some 60 million tonnes of rubbish is produced by 143 million Russians, with recycling a paltry 5%. Greenpeace has reported that 90 per cent of Moscow's waste goes to landfill and, after 25,000 people protested in late 2018 over toxic dumps, President Vladimir Putin signed a decree to create a federal recycling company in early 2019. Russia, the world's 73rd richest country, says it wants to process 80% of its waste by 2030, an ambitious goal.

Joint 21. Austria: 0.41 tonnes

Austria, where this waste incineration plant in Spittelau has been beautified, does not have such a beautiful record when it comes to waste, with its 8.6 million people producing almost five million tonnes of waste annually and recycling 26%. The world's 30th richest country is banning non-biodegradable plastic bags from next year and hopes to eliminate 7,000 tonnes of plastic waste a year.

Joint 21. Cyprus: 0.41 tonnes

Cyprus' environment minister last year said that 70% of Cypriot rubbish was going to landfill, compared to European directives of 10% or less, and Cyprus risks multi-million euro penalties if it does not clean up its act. Rising numbers of tourists are also putting pressure on the systems on the Mediterranean island, the world's 53rd richest country, to manage 541,000 tonnes of waste, of which just 13% is recycled.

Joint 21. Faroe Islands: 0.41 tonnes

The Faroe Islands, located in the North Atlantic between Iceland and Scotland and part of the Kingdom of Denmark, produces 61,000 tonnes of waste a year, or 1,25 tonnes per capita, but recycles over two-thirds of the archipelago's waste – the best rate of any of the 30 richest wasters. With little produce grown in the bitter climate, the Faroese import much of their fruit and vegetables – and have become experts in its conservation, which keeps food wastage to a minimum.

Joint 21. Greece: 0.41 tonnes

In 2016 the European Court fined debt-ridden Greece $11.3 million (£8.8m) for not following rules on disposing of rubbish. As much as 80% of waste was ending up at Greek landfill sites. The world's 74th richest country still produces almost 5.5 million tonnes of waste annually and recycles just 19%. Local paper Ekathimerini recently reported that almost half of waste sent to Greece's largest recycling plant, in Koropi, eastern Attica, was going to landfill.

20. Saudi Arabia: 0.43 tonnes

Saudi Arabia, the world's 22nd richest country, produces just over 16 million tonnes of waste a year, of which 15% is recycled. But although the kingdom is the least wasteful of the five Gulf countries on this list, it ranks number one in the world in food waste, according to a report by the Ministry of Environment, Water and Agriculture, throwing out 30% of all food produced.

19. Luxembourg: 0.45 tonnes

The Grand Duchy of Luxembourg, the world's fifth richest country, produces 356,000 tonnes of waste annually and recycles 28%, but still has a way to go to reduce its 0.45 tonnes of waste per person after recycling. Luxembourg only put a stop to free plastic bags in stores as of 2019 (a move made in the UK back in 2015), which it hopes will be a major driver in reducing single-use plastics.

18. Qatar: 0.46 tonnes

Qatar fares worse than its much larger neighbour Saudi Arabia. Even though it only produces one million tonnes of waste a year, a 16th of the kingdom's figure, it has an abysmal 3% recycling rate. The world's second richest country has been working hard at turning around its rubbish problem, however: total waste has declined by a third since 2011, with a focus on construction waste, and it aims to recycle 15% by 2022.

17. United Arab Emirates: 0.47 tonnes

Like its Gulf compatriots, the UAE is a wasteful country with a fast-rising population of nine million residents. The world's 13th richest produces 5.4 million tonnes of waste a year, recycling 20% (the best in the Gulf). A new federal law passed last year aims to increase recycling levels to 75%, with a punishing Dh1 million fine (£211,500) for illegal waste disposal. And in an innovative move, Dubai has sent a rubbish-eating 'shark' drone into its marina to pick up floating waste.

16. Israel: 0.48 tonnes

Israel, which produces 5.4 million tonnes of waste a year, also has the highest birth rate in the developed world. As a result disposable diapers make up a whopping 10% of its trash. The world's 54th richest country, which has a 25% recycling rate, says it is working with a leading nappy producer to try to develop the world's first nappy recycling plant.

Joint 14. Macau: 0.49 tonnes

At 14 and 13 respectively are China's two special administrative regions, Hong Kong and Macau. In Macau, local waste experts say more than half of the 378,000 annual tonnes of waste comes from the hotel industry; Macau receives 30 million tourists a year. The world's fourth richest country is also running out of residential space in its tiny 12 square miles, and is struggling to allow for enough waste plants or incinerators.

Joint 14. Switzerland: 0.49 tonnes

Think of Switzerland and you imagine fresh mountain air, not six million tonnes of waste. Although the world's 18th richest country recycles 32% of its waste, the country's recycling head says rising levels of consumerism are to blame for the sheer amount of waste produced. Most of the country has introduced a tax per bag of rubbish to try to keep waste down, but neighbours France and Germany still accuse Swiss 'rubbish tourists' of driving over the border to dump their trash.

13. Hong Kong: 0.51 tonnes

It is a similar story in the much larger region of Hong Kong, where the seven million residents produce almost six million tonnes of waste annually. While 34% is recycled, that still leaves 0.51 tonnes of MSW per person to manage, compared to mainland China's tiny 0.15 tonnes. Hong Kong is the 17th richest country in the world.

12. United States: 0.53 tonnes

The US, the world's 19th richest country, recycles more than a third of its 258 million tonnes of waste. But that still leaves 0.53 tonnes per person to be managed and, since China closed its doors to recycling, the rubbish has been mounting up. In 2017, China bought more than half of the scrap materials exported by the US. Some recycling plants now admit they have stopped sorting plastic and paper and are sending it straight to landfill.

11. Singapore: 0.54 tonnes

The world's seventh richest country also has one of the best recycling rates, at 61%, The island city-state turns most of its non-recyclable trash to ash, then ships it to a nearby nature reserve island. But Singapore has a big issue with plastic, its largest category of waste – almost none of which is recycled.

10. Canada: 0.56 tonnes

Canada, the world's 34th wealthiest country, produces 25 million tonnes of waste a year, or 0.56 tonnes per person (much of it plastic), and currently recycles 21%. But it is on a path to reform: its environment ministers last year announced ambitious goals to halve the country's waste within two decades, with zero waste plastic.

Joint 8. Denmark: 0.58 tonnes

Denmark, the world's 31st richest country, is seen as a very green country: it is illegal to send waste to landfill if it can be incinerated, and landfilled waste is hit with a tax of €62.56 (£55.25) per tonne. Yet it still produces almost 4.5 million tonnes of waste. More than a quarter is recycled today, and Denmark is on a serious recycling drive.

Joint 8. Malta: 0.58 tonnes

Malta, the world's 43rd richest country, has one of the lowest recycling rates in Europe at just 7%. It is one of the member states at risk of missing its 50% 2020 recycling targets, due to a lack of infrastructure and collection systems, coordination and incentives to prevent waste.

7. Bahrain: 0.61 tonnes

Bahrain, the world's 33rd richest country, is the smallest of the Gulf countries to appear on this list but the biggest waster. The 1.4 million residents produce almost 952,000 tonnes of waste: still 0.61 tonnes per person after just 8% is recycled. A rising population, limited land and fast industrialisation and urbanisation (Bahrain is the most densely populated country in the Gulf) has made waste management an issue. There is just one dump, the 700-acre Askar landfill site.

6. Iceland: 0.7 tonnes

Iceland's environment agency says Icelanders throw away a staggering amount of food and drink: 624lbs per person each year. The world's 25th richest country produces 231,000 tonnes of waste after recycling, or 0.7 tonnes per person. But Iceland, which sent 80% of waste to landfill in 1995, has been on a huge recycling drive and now has one of the highest recycling rates in the world, at 56% of all waste.

5. Guam: 0.73 tonnes

Guam, a US island territory in the West Pacific and the world's 56th richest country, has been struggling with waste management for more than a decade. Operations have been under federal receivership since 2008, after the Guam government failed to close the hazardous Ordot dump in 2008 and build a new landfill. It produces 141,500 tonnes of waste a year and recycles 18%, leaving 0.73 tonnes of waste per person to clear up.

4. Channel Islands: 0.78 tonnes

While the UK itself escapes the waste list, producing 0.35 tonnes of MSW per person after recycling annually, the Channel Islands (part of the British Isles) do not, producing almost 179,000 tonnes of waste annually. Guernsey, the second biggest of the Channel Islands, only got a waste plant last year; it was previously exporting waste to Sweden or sending it to landfill. Jersey is considered the 21st richest country in the world and Guernsey the 24th.

3. Cayman Islands: 0.8 tonnes

This British Overseas Territory and Caribbean paradise, the world's 40th richest country, produces 60,000 tonnes of waste annually – a tonne per person before recycling 21%. The 80ft George Town dump in Grand Cayman (ironically, the island's highest point) has been a public health issue for years, with toxic fires closing nearby schools and businesses. In 2017 plans for a modern waste management system were announced, although no date has yet been given to close the dump.

2. Monaco: 1.16 tonnes

European principality Monaco may make rubbish collection fun with hopscotch grids, but it has a major waste issue. The 46,000 tonnes generated by the tiny, ultra-wealthy population (where the per-capita income tops $100,000), and minute 5% recycling rate, means the world's third richest country has 1.16 tonnes per person to manage. Tourists increase the population tenfold each year, thanks to the Grand Prix and casinos, meaning all that rubbish is not coming from residents alone.

1. Bermuda: 1.24 tonnes

Bermuda, another British overseas territory and the sixth richest country in the world, is the biggest offender on our waste list. The 82,000 islanders on the British territory of Bermuda trash 1.24 tonnes of waste per person annually after recycling – and recycle a miniscule 2%. But the famed pink-sand beaches do have one massive problem: plastic pollution from the ocean washing up on shore. From 2022, Bermuda is completely banning single-use plastic in an attempt to clean up.

22 January 2019

'Drink and drop' – new survey reveals a nation of thirsty litterers

Research shows just what the nation is dropping.

A new report, produced by Keep Britain Tidy and commissioned by Defra, reveals just how much litter is being dropped and what it is.

The research reveals that the bulk of the litter that is being thoughtlessly thrown on our streets, parks and beaches is the result of our insatiable thirst for drinking on the go.

The survey, carried out at a representative sample of sites across the country in 2019, looked not only at the number of items dropped but at the volume of that litter and it revealed that almost three quarters of the litter – a staggering 75% was the result of drinks consumption.

The most littered item, by volume, was the small plastic bottle (up to 750ml) for non-alcoholic drinks, which accounted for 24.4% of the total, but these are joined by cans, larger bottles, glass bottles, coffee cups, takeaway soft drinks cups and cartons to create a mountain of waste, much of which could and should be recycled but is, instead, polluting our environment and costing millions of pounds to clean up.

Keep Britain Tidy Deputy CEO, Richard McIlwain, says: 'It's clear that our "food on the go" culture of convenience comes with real consequences, with food and drink packaging polluting our environment, which in turn costs millions to clean up and harms native wildlife and domestic pets.'

As we consider what a post-Covid green recovery should look like, we should allow ourselves to imagine a world without

litter and plastic pollution. It is clear that we urgently need new measures to tackle all types of littering but particularly to address the issue of drinks containers, which make up nearly three quarters of the volume of litter in this country.

This is why we need a well-designed and comprehensive deposit return scheme as soon as possible, for all sizes of plastic, glass and aluminium drinks containers. In more than 40 countries and regions around the world, such schemes can drive up collection rates for drinks containers to over 90%, creating clean material for recycling and reducing littering.

We are delighted that the Government is pressing ahead with plans to introduce a deposit return scheme for drinks bottles and cans in 2023 and government must ensure this timescale does not slip.

In addition, we are also calling for the introduction of a charge on single-use plastic and plastic-lined cups, including those use for take-away coffees and cold drinks. The charge on single-use plastic carrier bags reduced consumption by up to 90% and evidence suggests that a charge on single-use cups could in turn nudge us away from single use and towards a refill culture for drinks-on-the-go.

The research, carried out before the Coronavirus pandemic and subsequent lockdown, showed that despite the fall in the number of smokers over the past decade, cigarette butts are littered more than anything else, accounting for 66% of all litter items dropped.

The Government's own Environment Bill introduces the concept of extended producer responsibility (EPR), initially for packaging but with scope to encompass other products. EPR aims to make companies responsible for 100% of the net costs of dealing with the products when they become waste, which includes the cost of clearing up those products if littered.

'Given the prevalence of cigarette litter, we believe Government should ensure that EPR is applied to the tobacco industry, not just for cigarette packaging but for cigarette butts, which account for two-thirds of all littered items,' says Richard McIlwain.

To clean up this country, and to change the behaviour of those who, as we have seen so clearly in the past few weeks, think it is acceptable to pollute our beautiful parks and beaches with their rubbish, we need everyone to play their part and pay their fair share. Only then will we have an environment of which we can be proud.

9 June 2020

Litter and littering in England 2017 to 2018

Percentage of sites meeting acceptable standard for litter

86% to 96%

Cost of keeping the streets clean per household

£28

Most commonly found litter types

Percentage of people perceiving litter as a problem

30%

People engaged in doing something about litter

378,300 volunteers

Litter on the ground and site cleanliness

Usually, the more litter there is on the ground the greater the impact it has on how clean a place appears to be, which in turn can affect people's willingness to drop litter there. We use data from four sources to understand how much litter is found on the ground in England, and what types of items are most often found on our streets and beaches.

Measuring litter

There's no one perfect way to measure litter – for example:

♦ if we measured litter by weight, we wouldn't know if we were counting a small number of heavy items, or a large number of light items

♦ if we measured the number of litter items this wouldn't necessarily reflect the impact on the way a place looks – a small number of large items might make a place appear more littered than a large number of small items

♦ measuring only the presence or absence of litter does not show how long the litter has been there, or how much of it is present

How much litter is there?

Survey data from Keep Britain Tidy and the Association for Public Service Excellence (APSE)

Both Keep Britain Tidy, in their Local Environmental Quality Survey of England, and the Association for Public Service Excellence looked at the cleanliness of sites within England.

Sites are graded by their level of cleanliness:

♦ grade A meaning no litter is present

♦ grade B meaning - the area is predominantly free with some minor instances of litter

♦ grade C meaning widespread distribution of litter and refuse, with minor accumulations

♦ grade D meaning heavily affected with litter, with significant accumulations

Grades A and B are classed as meeting an acceptable standard.

As the sample selection differs between the two surveys, the percentage of sites meeting an acceptable level of cleanliness is shown as a range in the dashboard. For 2017 to 2018, this range is from 86% to 96%.

Keep Britain Tidy's data is based on an annual survey of site cleanliness based on a sample of sites which are designed to be representative geographically and of different levels of deprivation in England, based on the Index of Multiple Deprivation. The most recent survey, 2017 to 2018, covered 25 local authorities. In 2017 to 2018 the average number of sites that were graded as acceptable or higher was 86%.
Source: Keep Britain Tidy Litter in England survey 2017-2018

The Association of Public Service Excellence collects site cleanliness data from a number of local authorities who voluntarily provide the data. In 2017 to 2018 data was collected from 46 local authorities. Although the data was from a self-selecting sample of local authorities, the sample represented a range of geographical regions and levels of deprivation in England, based on the Index of Multiple Deprivation. In 2017 to 2018 the average number of sites that were graded as acceptable or higher was 96%.
Source: APSE Street Cleanliness Report

Great British Beach Clean data

Marine Conservation Society's (MCS) Great British Beach Clean is an annual beach clean, run in September, where volunteers, either individuals or groups, meet to collect litter from beaches. The data is recorded by the groups as they are collecting. The data is analysed to show how many items were present per 100 metres of beach. In the Great British Beach Clean 2017, in England, there were 911 items of litter per 100 metres. This compares to 802 items of litter per 100 metres in 2016.
Source: Marine Conservation Society

Reports made through the Love Clean Streets app

Around 2,700 people used the Love Clean Streets app to report litter incidents in the year ended 31 March 2018. In total they reported around 5,700 incidents of litter from 98 local authorities.
Source: BBits – Love Clean Streets, unpublished.

What type of litter is there?

Keep Britain Tidy - Litter in England survey 2017 to 2018

Data on the most commonly-found types of litter was recorded as part of Keep Britain Tidy's Litter in England survey. In 2018, smoking-related litter was the most commonly-found type of litter (79% of sites), followed by confectionery packs (60%) and non-alcoholic drinks-related (52%).

What type of litter is there?

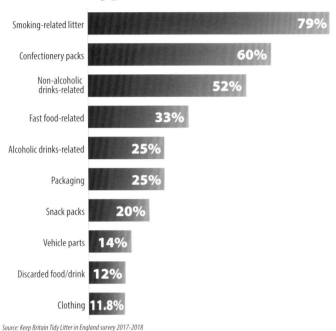

Source: Keep Britain Tidy Litter in England survey 2017-2018

Great British Spring Clean reports

All participants in the Great British Spring Clean (GBSC) are encouraged to report data on the types of litter they find. In 2018, the most commonly-found type of litter by participants in the Great British Spring Clean 2018 was non-alcoholic drinks-related (79% of participants), followed by alcoholic drinks-related (61%) and fast-food litter (54%).

What type of litter is there?

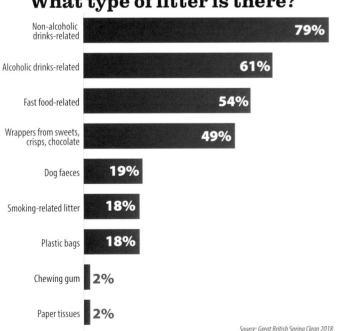

Source: Great British Spring Clean 2018

Great British Beach Clean

The Great British Beach Clean looks at type of litter found, and standardises it to how many items are found per 100 metres of beach. In 2017, in England, the top item found was small pieces of plastic and polystyrene (239 per 100 metres), then packets - crisps, sweets, lolly, sandwich (55 per 100 metres), then cigarette stubs (49 per 100 metres).

What type of litter is there?
How many items found
(per 100 metres of beach)

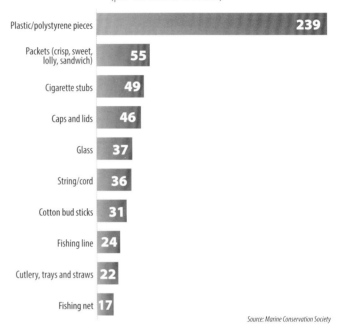

Source: Marine Conservation Society

How much does littering cost?

In 2017 to 2018 it cost local authorities £663 million or £28 per household to keep our streets clean. This figure does not include spending by other authorities whose role involves clearing litter, such as Highways England.

Source: MHCLG data

How big a problem do people think litter is?

In April 2017 to March 2018, 30 per cent of people in England said there was a very or fairly big problem with litter and rubbish in their area. This has been a fairly consistent picture with the figure changing little in recent years.

Source: Office for National Statistics

How engaged are people in doing something about it?

Around 371,000 people took part in the Great British Spring Clean throughout the UK, around 4,500 people took part in the Great British Beach Clean in England and 2,700 users reported litter via the Love Clean Streets App.

26 September 2019

'It was so gross, I nearly cried': Meet the UK's litter-picking army – fighting our rising tide of filth

Thousands of volunteers are trying to keep Britain clean as people go wild after lockdown. We join some in Bournemouth, as they face the discarded plastic, PPE, pants – and human poo.

By Sam Wollaston

On a promising July morning, Bournemouth's East Cliff limbers up for the day: dog walkers, power walkers, an outdoor gym class on a patch of grass. Four people in hi-vis vests beetle about purposefully, looking at the ground. They carry buckets and bags, and each has a tool – a stick with a handle at one end and a grabber at the other.

One of them, Lea Baker, 62, nimbly scales the clifftop fence to grab a Coke can. 'Sometimes, when there is a really difficult one and I get it, I'm like: "Yes, I win!"' she says, giving it a little fist pump.

Baker is a retired teacher, originally from Holland. 'I love England, but this is one aspect I hate,' she says, nodding at her bucket, now nearly full of cans and bottles, plastic, fag ends, wipes and other horrors. Cigarette butts are her bugbear. 'There are so many of them, and they take so long to pick up.' She's not a fan of dog poo either, tied up in plastic bags and then discarded or hung on the fence. 'It's actually better to leave the poo.'

Baker and her husband, Keith, are members of the Dorset Devils, a community litter-picking group operating on this part of the coast. Members volunteer to do their bit alongside the council to make their lovely part of the country less of a dump, as well as to get a bit of fresh air and exercise, generate community spirit and pride, and have a bit of a laugh.

They've been busier than ever since lockdown eased and people began to socialise outside. Not only is the volume of litter out of control, but the type of rubbish has brought a whole lot of new challenges, with personal protective equipment (PPE), nappies, wipes, tissues and human excrement just some of the horrid and hazardous things being left. All the Dorset Devils I meet refer to the two days during the heatwave last month when 500,000 people descended on this part of the south coast as 'the Invasion'. As front pages and TV news flashed images of Bournemouth beach full to bursting, the council was forced to declare a 'major incident', with traffic gridlocked, violent behaviour from visitors and emergency services stretched. The health secretary threatened to shut down the beaches if it continued.

Eight tonnes of rubbish was collected from the beach in the mile or so between Bournemouth pier and Boscombe pier on just one day. 'It was so gross, I nearly cried,' says Baker. 'Why can't they take it home?'

What you didn't get from the news was the smell, says Peter Ryan. Barbecues, burnt food, sun cream, alcohol, drugs and urine. Ryan, 61, is the founder of the Dorset Devils. He carries a sharps container as well as a bucket. You find a lot of used needles under Bournemouth pier. He has a top-of-the-range litter-picker, light and perfectly balanced; the Firebolt of litter-pickers. He emerges from a bush with a pair of men's underpants dangling from the end of it. 'There you go, Sam … your size, I think.'

Why do they do it? 'Because we love where we live, we care and we want to make a difference out there,' he says. 'The litter-picking community is annoyed, disappointed and disillusioned that a minority of people have simply reverted to their poor manners and behaviours. It's never acceptable to trash any environment – bin it or take it home.'

The reopening of the fast food outlets: that's the moment it got really bad

Still, the Invasion has been good for recruitment: 60 new devils signed up in its aftermath. There are now 584 volunteers, ranging in age from four to 84.

And it's not just in Dorset. Andrew Wood, who started a Facebook group, UK Litterpicking Groups, estimates there are about 2,000 groups between Land's End and John o'Groats, taking in beaches, city parks, canals in the Midlands and mountains in Wales and Scotland. 'I reckon you've probably got 100,000 people litter-picking across the UK in the course of a week, and that is an army,' he says, on the phone from Hereford. 'Because we hate to see it, we are disgusted with the mess.' He pinpoints the moment when the litter increased dramatically after the easing of lockdown. 'The reopening of the fast food outlets: that's the moment it got really bad.'

Richard McIlwain, the deputy chief executive of Keep Britain Tidy, says all the park managers he has spoken to say this summer is the worst they have ever known for litter. He thinks it may have something to do with festival culture. 'There are always photographs after festivals showing a sea of discarded tents, barbecues, rubbish. Single-use culture has just transferred into parks because, obviously, none of those festivals are on,' he says. 'I think there is also some psychology in the way people behave post-lockdown. The sense of freedom means some of the social norms go out of the window.'

A litter-pick in my local park in north-west London, with my two boys, using equipment borrowed from the Friends of Gladstone Park group, produces sacks full of nitrous oxide

canisters and other drug-taking paraphernalia, as well as bottles and cans, takeaway packaging, another pair of men's underpants, bagged dog poo and unbagged human poo (which we felt neither qualified nor inclined to deal with). Plus a ton of disposable gloves and masks. Why, when you wear a mask to protect others as well as yourself, do you then drop it on the ground, potentially endangering people? Why, when we city-dwellers have come to appreciate our parks like never before, do we then thoroughly trash them?

Covid-19 has been a major contributor. Not just PPE, but more things in supermarkets, such as baked goods, getting individually wrapped; coffee shops no longer accepting reusable cups; and pubs serving takeaway beers in plastic cups. It's all been a step backwards in the journey towards reuse. Then you've got public toilets being closed, and the small matter of local authorities being stretched to breaking point. And staycationing will mean UK beauty spots are going to take even more of a hammering.

The rubbish epidemic has spread beyond beaches and urban parks. The National Trust this weekend warned of an increase in 'fly camping', where visitors pitch a tent illegally and leave all their rubbish, and sometimes even their tents, behind. Remember the wheelie suitcase complete with tent, clothes, towels, tissues and other rubbish left by a tarn in the Lake District a few weeks ago? Andrea Hall is an artist and open water swimmer in her native Yorkshire. She has noticed 'shedloads' more litter recently by the banks of the lakes and rivers she swims in, in the water, lurking in the riverbeds below her. As lockdown eases and the weather's good, there's 'a deluge of people who just come into these places and leave them a tip. It's us who go around afterwards and pick it up.'

Hall was so incensed she made a poster, free to download, of a swimmer getting hit on the head by a discarded drinks can, with the line: 'Don't Be a Tosser'. York city council used the same line on one of its campaigns; they tell it like it is in Yorkshire.

So what can be done? Wood would like to see more enforcement. 'A nice, hefty fine of 100 quid helps deter someone from chucking their McDonald's wrappers out of the window,' he says.

McIlwain says local authorities need more money. And they need to put some temporary toilets into parks – some of the portable ones that aren't going to festivals, perhaps. He talks of extending producer responsibility, making manufacturers responsible for the costs of waste management, which would encourage them to use more reusable packaging. He also salutes the 100,000-strong army of litter-pickers. 'If the litterers are a visible expression of the people who don't care, then the pickers are a visible expression of the people who do.' Imagine what the country would look like without them.

Back in Bournemouth, we have come down on to the beach, the scene of the Invasion a couple of weeks ago. We hook up with some more Dorset Devils, including brothers Sam and Ollie Gell, aged 11 and 10. 'It's something to do, and it's good for the environment,' says Sam. Olly says it's a bit like playing hide-and-seek. Both would rather be picking up litter on the beach than at school. Plus, they get a bubble-gum-flavoured ice-cream from their nan for their efforts.

The beach isn't too bad today, for a Monday after a sunny weekend. The council have already been through, with their machines that sift through the sand. Just a few fag ends for Baker to pick up. She goes missing for a while, and we wonder where she has gone. Then, we hear a cry of dismay from behind a beach hut. It's something horrible …

And, oh dear lord! It's huge, and covered in flies, and there is no excuse for it; the toilet just up the path on the clifftop is now open. This one is going nowhere, I'm afraid. No winners, no fist pump from Baker. Just a look of despair and revulsion. 'We have our limits,' she says.

21 July 2020

'Beaches and parks are overwhelmed with rubbish – it's heartbreaking': Littering has soared during lockdown

Has Britain really become a nation of litter louts overnight? It seems unlikely, but the pandemic has changed people's behaviour.

By Harry Wallop

The quantity of Ocado bags under my kitchen sink has now become so voluminous that I may suffocate under a sea of plastic, long before coronavirus gets me. The online supermarket used to religiously take back any plastic bags (not just its own) to be recycled, but at the start of the Covid crisis it paused this 'following World Health Organisation advice'. The online supermarket cannot say when it will restart recycling.

It is just one small, and admittedly very middle class, example of how the battle against single-use plastics has been abandoned in our war against the pandemic. But it is not the only one.

Two public water fountains I pass each day – both installed in my neighbourhood – have been wrapped up in bin liners and red-and-white warning tape, as if they were biohazards. My local café no longer accepts reusable cups for you to take your coffee away in.

Rubbish on the streets and at the beach

The surge in domestic recycling, as consumers stayed at home and ordered takeaways and Amazon parcels, meant some councils just could not cope. Cardiff started burning household recycling, saying it was the only way of maintaining a kerbside collection during lockdown.

Worst of all are the scenes at beaches and parks, overwhelmed in disposable plastic bottles, nitrous oxide canisters, bags, face masks and food containers, as people emerge from lockdown determined to let their hair down. 'The scenes of litter are absolutely heartbreaking,' says Natalie Fee, environmental campaigner and founder of the City to Sea not-for-profit organisation, which tries to stop plastic pollution.

Last Thursday, the hottest day of the year so far, 11 tonnes of litter was collected from Brighton beach – the most cleaning staff had collected in a single day. The average at this time of year is around three tonnes, the local council said. Richard McIlwain, deputy chief executive of the anti-litter charity Keep Britain Tidy, says: 'We're hearing from park managers it is the worst they have ever faced.'

Has Britain really become a nation of litter louts overnight? It seems unlikely, but Kirstie Allsopp – a long-term ambassador for Keep Britain Tidy – believes the pandemic has changed people's behaviour.

A shift in responsibility

'I think it's particularly happening now because there's been this strange shift in responsibility', she tells me. 'During the Covid crisis, the government took over and told us where we could go, how to be. If they are telling us how to behave, why have they not provided us with bins to throw our stuff away?

'As a nation we have to take responsibility for our own actions. Don't presume your picnic is anybody else's responsibility.'

There is, of course, a logic to why there is so much rubbish in parks and beaches. Lizzie Prior, beachwatch officer at the Marine Conservation Society, says: 'There are very few cafes or establishments to go to. People are coming prepared with food and drink, but unfortunately leaving it there. It is worrying.'

Some point out that the pictures of litter are misleading, however. It is simply a matter of all our litter being concentrated into a relatively small and very visible area: public parks and beaches. Travel into any city centre and rubbish levels have dropped significantly.

Less rubbish, but less recycling

Richard Kirkman, chief technology and innovation officer at Veolia, the waste and recycling company, says: 'Overall, across the country, there has been a little bit less rubbish in recent months. Because industry and commerce has stopped.' He says the data isn't yet verified, but the 20 million tonnes of annual commercial waste has reduced by about 45 per cent. And though household and parks waste has increased a lot, it hasn't gone up enough to offset the decline in factory and office waste.

Even if overall rates of litter are not increasing, many are worried that litter from office or school canteens – usually recycled – is now being displaced in parks and beaches. 'Here, it will invariably be incinerated,' says McIlwain of Keep Britain Tidy. 'About half of local authorities don't even bother with on-street recycling bins. Those that do suffer from rates of contamination of between 10 per cent and 90 per cent. Most of what's been collected from parks and beaches will be incinerated or go to landfill.'

Allsopp believes that for all the hard work Keep Britain Tidy does, its logo – the 'Tidyman' binning a piece of rubbish – is problematic when park and beach bins are full. 'Litter begets litter. If you see someone else leaving their rubbish to the side of a bin [because it is full], you don't feel so bad leaving it. We ought now to be saying "don't bin it, take it home."

McIlwain agrees that if you can be bothered to lug your picnic to the beach, you should be bothered to take the empty – and far lighter – packaging home with you to recycle.

What happened to the Blue Planet effect?

The question is whether this is a short-term blip, or a worrying reversal of the Blue Planet effect, which encouraged many more consumers to reuse and recycle?

'We can't underestimate the power of the plastics industry and how they see this as an opportunity to push their agenda,' says Fee at City to Sea. 'They are using public health and safety as an excuse push back against all the progress we've made.' In the USA, the plastics industry lobbied to reverse the ban on single-use plastic bags, arguing plastic bags were the 'most sanitary choice'.

She remains optimistic, however. Last week, 119 experts, including virologists and epidemiologists, from 18 countries – coordinated by Greenpeace – concluded reusable containers pose no threat to the public. Costa, Britain's coffee chain, has started to allow customers to bring in their own cups once again.

'People have spent a lot of lockdown outside, connecting with nature,' says Fee. 'Time has run out and people are far more aware of that. People now realise there is a connection between plastic and climate change.'

The litter may be selfish. But it is not conclusive proof Britain has stopped caring about the environment.

2 July 2020

The decomposition of waste in landfills

A story of time and material.

By Rick Leblanc

From a sustainability perspective, it's important to know how long it takes various types of garbage to decompose. We should focus our efforts especially on reducing the consumption of products that generate waste materials that take a long time to completely break down.

Let's review how long it takes for various waste categories to decompose in landfills, along with some relevant statistics.

The rate of decomposition can depend on landfill conditions.

Plastic waste

Plastic products are very common in our modern life. According to the Pacific Institute, we used approximately 17 million barrels of oil just for producing plastic water bottles in 2006. Plastic waste is one of many types of wastes that take too long to decompose. Normally, plastic items can take up to 1,000 years to decompose in landfills. Even plastic bags we use in our everyday life take anywhere from 10 to 1,000 years to decompose, and plastic bottles can take 450 years or more.

Disposable diapers

In the United States alone, about 3.3 million tons of disposable diapers were thrown away in 2018. These disposable diapers take approximately 250-500 years to decompose in landfills, thus underscoring the importance of programs offering diaper and absorbent hygiene product recycling.

Aluminium cans

About 42.7 billion aluminium cans, over 81,000 cans per minute, were recycled in America in 2019. But, at the same time, in every three-month period in the U.S., enough aluminium cans and packaging are thrown away – 2.66 billion tons in 2018 – to rebuild the entire American commercial air fleet. Aluminium cans take 80-100 years in landfills to completely decompose.

Glass

Glass is normally very easy to recycle due to the fact that it's made of sand. By simply breaking down the glass and melting it, we can produce new glass. But the shocking fact is that if glass is thrown away in landfills, it takes a million years to decompose. And according to some sources, it doesn't decompose at all.

Paper waste

Paper is the largest element in American municipal solid waste. Normally, it takes two to six weeks in a landfill to get completely decomposed, but can take decades, depending on moisture levels within the landfill. Recycling paper items saves a lot of landfill space while also reducing the energy and virgin material usage demanded by making non-recycled paper.

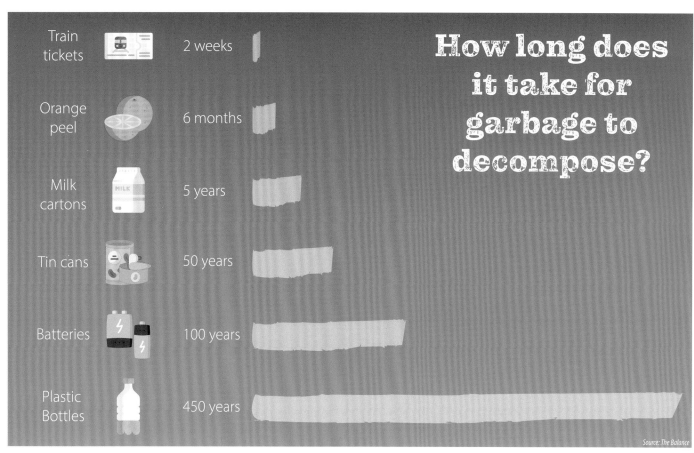

Train tickets — 2 weeks

Orange peel — 6 months

Milk cartons — 5 years

Tin cans — 50 years

Batteries — 100 years

Plastic Bottles — 450 years

How long does it take for garbage to decompose?

Source: The Balance

Other waste items

Different sources have different information on the actual time various waste items take to decompose. Here are some estimates for common waste items

Waste Item	Decomposition Time
Cigarette butts	10-12 years
Monofilament fishing line	600 years
Rubber boot soles	50-80 years
Foamed plastic cups	50 years
Leather shoes	25-40 years
Milk cartons	5 years
Plywood	1-3 years
Cotton gloves	3 months
Cardboard	2 months
Styrofoam	Does not biodegrade
Nylon fabric	30-40 years
Tin can	50 years
Ropes	3-14 months
Aluminium cans	80-100 years
Train tickets	2 weeks
Batteries	100 years
Sanitary pads	500-800 years
Wool clothing	1-5 years
Tinfoil	Does not biodegrade

Source: The Balance

Food waste

Food is the second largest waste item in American landfills. The time taken for food waste decomposition depends on the type of food. Normally, an orange peel takes six months, while an apple core takes around two months, and a banana peel takes two to 10 days to decompose. Composting and food waste recycling are great ways to divert food waste away from landfills.

Final note

The increasing volume of waste is a major concern for humans and the environment. The best way to deal with this problem is to avoid products that generate waste materials that take more than a year to decompose in landfills. Every household and organization should also have a proactive plan for recycling to divert more materials away from the waste stream.

16 January 2021

Why is landfill so bad?

Why is landfill so bad?

To strive towards a cleaner, greener and more sustainable future, we need to face the issues that are challenging us today. As a nation of consumers, we are forever buying new products, over-filling our fridges and opting for quick, cheap buys that have short life spans. Though many companies are taking huge strides to combat this by offering recyclable alternatives, landfills are still one of our biggest problems and one that has disastrous consequences for our planet. And as landfills are paid for by the council, it's often the taxpayer who foots the bill.

What is landfill?

A landfill is, quite simply, a plot of land that's used to dump waste. Think about a sea of broken, foul smelling rubbish that has been buried and left to rot for years on an unused piece of land — it's not a pretty sight.

What's worse is, that junk is not going anywhere.

For most households and businesses in the UK, there is a disconnection between waste and the impacts it has on the Earth. When we throw out our trash, a waste disposal truck will come along and take it away and, just like that, our bins are nice and empty again. Out of sight, out of mind.

But, unfortunately, it's not as simple as that.

What happens to waste at a landfill?

A landfill is a man-made structure that is either built into the earth or on top of it. It's designed to be isolated from rain, air and groundwater. The purpose of this is to stop waste coming into contact with the surrounding environment, however, a lack of oxygen causes a bacterial reaction and rubbish begins to break down and decay, albeit incredibly slowly. This, in turn, produces gases and liquids including methane and leachate.

Methane is highly flammable and can cause some serious damage if allowed to build up underground. It's also one

of the largest contributors to greenhouse gases and, thus, a culprit of climate warming. Many landfills have pipes that collect the methane, which is then sent to be burnt off for energy. However, the environmental damage far outweighs any energy that is produced.

As mentioned, landfills produce gases such as methane and CO2. Because the waste is trapped without oxygen, even natural produce such as fruit and vegetables can take a long time to break down.

Landfills also produce landfill leachate. A liquid that seeps through rubbish, often collecting toxic substances along the way. If not carefully managed, leachate can threaten both surface and ground water, contaminating water supplies and the local environment.

As Earth's population rises, so does our waste consumption, meaning the devastating consequences that landfill has on the environment will increase if we continue to use them the way that we do.

The UK produced 222.9 million tonnes of waste in 2016 and, up until 2018, around two-thirds of plastic waste was sent to China. This gives you an indication of the vast scale of our waste and how much the UK requires a sophisticated waste and recycling management system that is fit for purpose and sustainable.

Landfill sites in the UK

There are around 500 landfill sites in the UK, with the majority of them located in England. Many people probably don't know where their nearest site is located, which makes it harder to see landfill as a problem. Around 35 million tonnes of rubbish lay there.

The largest landfill in the UK was the renowned Pakington site situated just outside of Birmingham. Instead of using an underground method, this one quite literally towered rubbish and covered 380 acres of land. Now closed, it's covered in clay and soil and the long, slow process of breakdown has begun.

Landfill laws

Modern landfills have tight restrictions and the UK sits under the Landfill Directive, an EU law. This orders local councils to minimise organic and garden waste going to landfill (a huge CO2 contributor) and encourages them to use alternative waste-disposal methods.

Landfill and business

For business and industries, it is against the law to send hazardous and non-hazardous waste to the same landfill and they are responsible for finding alternative means of disposal. It is also obligatory to fill out a waste transfer note when handing over rubbish to a registered waste management organisation such as your recycling company or scrap metal merchant.

The solution: zero to landfill

So, now it's clear why landfill is so bad, it's time to consider the alternatives. More and more businesses are cutting down on unnecessary waste and recycling where they can.

Zero to landfill is, as the name suggests, a way of managing waste without it ever ending up in a landfill. This is achieved through the use of recycling, reusing, green technology and waste-to-energy. At First Mile, we provide a 100% zero-to-landfill solution. In other words, we are passionate about avoiding damage to the environment at all costs.

Recycling

Most people already do this without thinking. Recycling has become part of our lives and we can only encourage businesses to do it more effectively. We offer a whole choice of recycling solutions, from food waste to coffee cups, electronics to coffee grounds. You name it; we'll handle it. It's as simple as that.

Reusing

Before throwing something out, consider how you might reuse it and give it a new lease of life. Can you use packaging such as cardboard boxes and shredded paper again? Can you get your computers repaired and upgraded without chucking them away? We tend to throw things away prematurely, so make sure to stop and think before you do.

Green technology

Green technology is a way of tracking your CO2 emissions and your environmental impact so that you can reduce waste at the source. By understanding your energy usage, you'll be able to manage and save without ever being wasteful.

Waste-to-energy

Unfortunately, not everything can be recycled. As you know, landfills do have a way of producing energy from methane, but this does not align with our zero-to-landfill ethos.

Instead, your waste is taken to an energy-to-waste facility. Here, your rubbish is safely incinerated and generates electricity and heat that are used to power homes. For remnants that can't be burned, they are packed down into building materials. Voila!

23 September 2020

Out of sight...

Out of mind?

The UK will burn more than half its rubbish as it doubles the number of incinerators over next 10 years

Opponents claim the boom will increase air pollution, exacerbate climate change and threaten much-needed recycling.

By Tom Bawden

The UK faces a wave of protests as the number of incinerators used to burn rubbish is set to more than double within a decade.

The waste incineration boom will increase air pollution, exacerbate climate change and threaten much-needed recycling, opponents claim.

The 44 waste incinerators across the UK burned 10.9 million tonnes of rubbish last year, much of it in England, where it accounted for 42 per cent of rubbish disposal.

Incineration will soon account for more than half of all waste disposal, data shows.

Sixteen new incinerators are under construction, which will increase burning capacity by more than a third. A further 45 incinerators have been approved but haven't started building and 40 more are at planning stages.

Figures 'extremely concerning'

Green Party MP Caroline Lucas said: 'These figures are extremely concerning. Burning our rubbish marks a failure of policy and imagination on the part of the Government and local councils.'

Critics say the rise is alarming because incineration plants cause air pollution, harming health, and increase carbon dioxide emissions which exacerbate climate change. Incinerators could also reduce recycling by encouraging councils to burn more waste, they say.

This threat is acute since China, where most British waste was typically sent, has banned imports of plastic, paper and card – and Brexit may shut off a further major waste destination.

42% of waste burned

Incinerators burn huge amounts of the UK's rubbish. Last year, 42 per cent of the country's plastic, paper, cardboard and other waste was burned – generating heat and electricity in the process.

Their growth has been phenomenal. In 2006, most waste was sent to landfill, with 3.3 million tonnes – or just over 10 per cent of UK waste – being incinerated.

A decade or so later, taxes that were introduced on landfill as available land shrank have made burning the much cheaper option, leading to the number of incinerators more than doubling, to 44, since 2010. The plans mean that 100 more have been proposed.

China no longer taking waste

Traditionally, the UK has sent about two thirds of its waste to be recycled in China, which has now banned imports. Much of this had been diverted to Malaysia, which is now introducing its own ban. And another major source of our waste – Europe – may also be blocked after Brexit.

All this waste has to go somewhere – and the UK's recycling infrastructure is already stretched – so it seems likely that much of the rubbish that went overseas will now be

Investigation into recyclable waste being wrongly incinerated

Brighton and Hove Council has launched an investigation into waste incineration after a binman claimed tonnes of rubbish meant for recycling had been burnt after Christmas.

Ken Quantick said he was collecting eight tonnes of recycling a day which was wrongly being incinerated, as the site operator Veolia became swamped by a huge volume of waste after Christmas.

'I'm so disgusted by it'

'We work one of nine routes and suddenly they started telling my team of three workers to start dumping our recycling in general household waste which is destined to be incinerated.

'I questioned them and they said our loads was listed as contaminated but I've been working 14 years and this has never happened before,' Mr Quantick said.

'Residents think their rubbish is being recycled but it isn't. People are carefully picking out paper, plastic and tins only for the recycling firm to burn it. It's a public scandal and I'm so disgusted by it that I can't stand by and stay silent any longer,' he said.

'Completely untrue'

A council spokesman said: 'We know there is an issue concerning contamination at the Veolia site. We have launched an investigation and are speaking to Veolia and our own staff about the situation.

'However, claims that Veolia is burning recycling because the plant is overwhelmed are completely untrue,' he added.

A spokesman for Veolia said: 'Loads might be rejected if it is deemed to contain too high levels of contamination. This is to protect the quality of our end recycled product and ensure the best environmental performance.'

burned. The government has held out the prospect of an 'incineration tax', which could curb some of that demand.

As well as exports, some 12.5 per cent of waste currently goes to landfill, and much of that is likely to be diverted to incinerators as well in the coming years. But while incineration causes air pollution and exacerbates climate change, that doesn't mean continuing with landfill is a good option. It takes up valuable land and can leak methane if not properly sealed – though the waste can potentially be dug up and reused at a later date.

How polluting incinerators actually are

There are also questions over just how polluting incinerators are. A study for Public Health England by researchers at Imperial College London and King's College London did find evidence of 'particulate' pollution around the incinerators but said concentrations were 'very low'.

However, the research didn't look at even smaller particulates – or the carbon dioxide produced by burning fossil fuels such as plastic (made from oil).

Another study, involving an analysis of official data by the campaign group the UK Without Incineration Network, found that the country's incinerators collectively produce the same amount of 'particulate' air pollution over the course of a year as 250,000 working lorries.

Industry body the Environmental Services Association disputed that report, and the Environment Agency have figures.

Incinerators produce only 0.03 per cent of PM10 particulates and 0.05 per cent of PM2.5 particulates. This compares to 5.35 per cent/4.96 per cent from traffic and 22.4 per cent/34.3 per cent from wood fires and stoves in people's houses.

Meanwhile, incinerators produce 1.12 per cent of nitric oxide and nitrogen dioxide – higher than the 0.57 per cent from domestic wood and stove burning, but well below the 33.5 per cent from traffic.

'Was that the best you could come up with?'

Oxford University's Professor Peter Edwards, said: 'The increase can only ever be justified as a temporary solution otherwise future generations will say "Was that the best you could come up with to solve such a massive problem?"

Friends of the Earth campaigner Julian Kirby added: 'Incinerators hamper efforts to reduce, reuse and recycle by forcing councils to supply rubbish.'

Shlomo Dowen, of the campaign group UK Without Incineration Network, said: 'There is no excuse for building new incinerators. They are harming recycling and costing the public hundreds of millions of pounds that could be better spent.'

Proponents say it generates heat and energy

The Environmental Services Association, which represents waste companies, refutes the criticism because the burning is used to generate heat and electricity, known as Energy from Waste.

'The current main alternative is landfill, but Energy from Waste generates electricity and heat…[and] is one of the most tightly regulated industries in the power sector,' a spokeswoman said.

Public Health England found no evidence of adverse health impacts associated with living near incinerators, she said.

Opponents criticised the study, saying it didn't measure for smaller, more damaging, particles.

A government spokesman said: 'Waste incineration is the best management option for waste that cannot be prevented, reused or recycled. It plays an important role in landfill diversion, reducing its environmental impact. Our strategy commits to increasing the efficiency of energy for waste plants.'

11 January 2019

31 Facts you wish you didn't know about plastic waste

Look around you, how much plastic can you see right now?

Chances are you're drinking from a coffee cup which might be plastic coated, using a plastic phone case. Even the pen on your desk is almost certainly plastic.

Plastic today really does make the world go around.

However, over the coming years things will have to change.

Thanks to things like the 'David Attenborough effect', many people are starting to really understand the impact of plastic waste and have been influenced to make a change.

Governments are banning single use plastics around the world, and many companies are trying to pre-empt this by introducing bans themselves such as Guinness banning any plastic from their packaging.

Shops from Iceland to Ikea are making moves to drastically reduce their disposable plastics over the coming years. Meanwhile, Kenya has imposed the toughest plastic bag ban yet, charging up to $38,000 or 4 years in jail for using them.

1. A report in the Guardian has estimated that 8.3 billion tons of plastic have been produced since the 1950s, the equivalent in weight of more than 800,000 Eiffel Towers.

2. Only about 30% of plastic ever produced is still in use. The remainder has been disposed of...

3. The 70% of plastic waste that has been disposed of can be broken down as follows: 79% is either in landfills or in the environment, 12% has been incinerated and 9% has been recycled

4. Attempting to recycle plastic might not be as sustainable as you once thought. Many rich countries have been sending their plastic waste to poorer countries where it will likely end up in landfills instead of being recycled.

5. Plastic takes thousands of years to decompose. In the process, it breaks down into thousands of microplastics that can be ingested and enter the food cycle.

6. If you build separate systems for plastic recycling, that's additional pollution caused in the construction, transportation, cleaning and filtering of waste.

7. The level of plastic used is increasing unabated. Half of all plastic made since 1950 was produced in the last 13 years.

8. One geological indicator of the Anthropocene (the new geological period we are in, as indicated by modern man's impact on a changing environment) will be the levels of waste in the ground.

9. Plastic can now be found on every beach in the world, from busy tourist beaches to isolated island paradises.

10. The world's population of 2.5 billion produced 1.5 million tonnes of plastic in 1950. Today this figure is over 320 million tonnes, and is set to double by 2034.

11. By 2050, there will likely be more plastic in the sea than fish if we carry on at our current trajectory.

12. Every day around 8 million pieces of plastic finds its way into our oceans.

13. Some estimates suggest there is now around 5.25 trillion pieces of plastic on our oceans.

14. Of this 5.25 trillion tonnes of plastic in our oceans, only 269,000 tonnes are floating on the surface, while some 4 billion microfibres per square kilometre litter the deep sea. This is the equivalent of 1345 adult blue whales, and 500 times the number of stars in our galaxy.

15. The strength and flexibility which makes plastic so useful also means that it lasts for hundreds of years in our environment. A plastic bottle will take over 450 years to break down, and when it does it will slowly disintegrate into thousands of tiny micro plastics. That means that every piece of plastic you have ever used is still in the environment today.

16. One study estimated that it would take 67 ships 1 year to clean up less than 1% of the Great Pacific Garbage Patch. That doesn't even consider the majority of plastic which has sunk to the ocean floors.

17. It is no longer a question of if we can tolerate plastic, but how bad it is to human health. The average person now eats around 70,000 pieces of microplastic each year. This is the equivalent to 100 bits of microplastic per meal, according to a study by Environmental Pollution. If you think you can cleverly avoid this, you are sadly mistaken,

as a team of UK-based researchers found that 14 pieces of microplastic had accumulated next to their dinner plates within just 20 minutes by placing petri dishes with sticky surfaces next to dinner plates.

18. One study found marine plastic pollution in 100% of marine turtles, 59% of whales, 40% of seabirds and 36% of seals examined.

19. This is not just a problem that affects poorer countries. Approximately 5,000 items of plastic pollution have been found per mile of the beaches here in the UK.

20. Believe it or not, over 150 plastic bottles litter each mile of the UK's beaches.

21. The effects plastic has on marine life is devastating. Around 100,000 marine mammals and turtles are killed by plastic pollution each year, as well as 1 million sea birds.

22. By 2050, virtually every seabird on the planet will have eaten plastic.

23. Nearly one million plastic bottles are sold every minute around the world. Sadly this figure is due to increase by 20% by 2050. The rate of increase is exponential, the findings showing that in 2016 more than 480 billion plastic bottles were purchased compared to 300 billion just ten years before. Of this, just 7% were recycled into new bottles, the rest ending up in landfills.

24. Nearly half of all plastic rubbish generated globally is due to packaging. This shows the importance to try to buy consumable goods that are plastic free.

25. Nearly 40% of plastic is only used once before it is thrown away.

26. A shocking but sadly true figure, according to Ecowatch, is that between 500 billion and 1 trillion plastic bags are used worldwide every year. A large city like New York alone uses 23 billion plastic bags annually, according to the New York City Department of Environmental Conservation. Fortunately, something is at least being done to reduce this number, as a bill has just been introduced to ban plastic grocery bags.

27. The World Economic Forum has found that just 10 rivers across Asia and Africa carry 90% of the plastic that ends up in the oceans. Eight of these rivers are in Asia, the Yangtze, Indus, Yellow, Hai He, Ganges, Pearl, Amur, and Mekong, and two are in Africa, the Nile and the Niger. This is due to high populations living in areas with poor waste management systems.

28. The average time that a plastic bag is used for is just 12 minutes. And they take up to a thousand years to decompose!

29. If you lined up the plastic thrown away each year, it would be enough to circle the earth four times.

30. Plastic production uses around 8% of the world's oil production.

31. The plastic that does float is likely to be carried to one of five ocean patches. The biggest of these is the Great Pacific Garbage Patch, located between Hawaii and California. It is twice the size of Texas, or 3 times the size of France, and outnumbers sea life six to one.

If you are feeling overwhelmed by these facts, a lot can be done to reduce your plastic consumption.

Start by trying to shop plastic free. We have put together a list of the UK's best plastic free online shops to help you on this journey.

Admittedly this journey towards reducing your plastic waste is not easy. Read about our first steps towards plastic free supermarket shopping.

Even if you only take small steps today, you will be making a difference.

13 October 2019

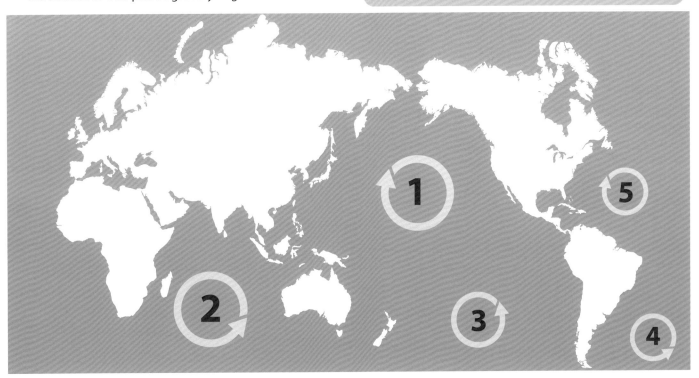

Our problems with plastic

We need a holistic approach to material use.

By Liz Lee Reynolds

Plastic pollution has rapidly become one of the biggest issues of recent years, with many now trying to significantly reduce their plastic waste.

Millions of tonnes of plastic find their way into the ocean every year, creating a garbage patch in the Pacific twice the size of Texas. The UK alone goes through an estimated 3.7 million tonnes of plastic a year and in 2015 only a third of this was recycled.

Plastic products can take over 400 years to decompose and as they do the plastic particles left behind continue to cause damage. Hundreds of thousands of these microparticles enter the food chain every year, along with any toxic chemicals attached to them.

Carbon footprint

A new report by the Green Alliance has shown the clear issues in how supermarkets and brands are responding to the customer demand for less plastic. Often alternatives such as glass, metal and paper have a much higher carbon footprint, particularly if they are still single-use items.

The report detailed, for instance, that the paper bags often used instead of plastic ones in supermarket bakery aisles are just as quickly disposed of, but producing them uses four times as much energy.

Morrison's has chosen to replace its plastic grocery bags with paper alternatives, but these would have to be used 43 times to beat a plastic counterpart on lower environmental impact.

This may even present a reverse trend as in recent years many consumers, encouraged by the 5p charges, had begun to move to reusing their plastic shopping bags and may immediately think that they don't need to do the same with a paper alternative.

The Green Alliance report showed a worrying tendency for supermarkets and other manufacturers to not fully consider and assess the environmental impact of plastic alternatives and instead opt for knee jerk removal.

Disposability

It is shocking how quickly plastic became an everyday staple in the modern world. In the little over 100 years it has existed its presence has seeped into almost every minute of our lives.

It was only in the 1950s that plastic really started to take off. With a rapidly growing consumer culture, it is easy to see the attraction of this material.

It's lightweight but durable, easy to clean, flexible (making its uses almost endless) and, above all, relatively inexpensive to produce.

When we look at the products we will use over and over again these virtues shine out. A hardy set of reusable containers could last a family their whole lifetime, and even be passed through generations if well cared for, although these cheap products are rarely seen as a family heirloom in the same way that a glass bowl might be.

This is part of plastic's problem. The cheap material is not readily made into cherishable items and instead creates mounds of highly durable tat that is disposed of without a second thought.

Sustainable alternative?

There are, however, ways for plastic to be positively used and this presents our second problem with plastic: our complete aversion to the stuff.

In the last few weeks, around 7 million real Christmas trees will have been disposed of in the UK. Although there are environmentally friendly methods of doing this, it is a sad fact that many of these trees will end up in landfill.

If you buy an artificial tree it will take only 10 years of use for it to be less carbon intensive than its soil-grown cousin and a good quality artificial tree can easily last a family for decades.

While there are clearly reusable and durable products which utilise the benefits of plastic, the more significant issue is the single use, disposable plastics which are currently choking the oceans.

However, there still needs to be a level of scrutiny of the alternatives offered. Bamboo coffee cups, for instance, quickly became a popular alternative to disposable cups which nearly always come with a plastic lid and coating on the cup.

These bamboo cups are supposedly made from a sustainable alternative, however, the bamboo fibres are held together by a plastic glue. The glue is not intended to be exposed to high temperatures, and the boiling water needed to make your favourite hot beverage means that hazardous plastic particles are being released into the drink.

Holistic approach

As well as being bad for health, these cups are often not so easily disposed of as the manufacturers claim. It is difficult to separate the bamboo fibre and the glue when it comes to recycling. Instead, it is likely the cup will end up as another product in landfill.

The issue with our plastic use and with popular alternatives stem from the same impulse towards easy solutions.

Consumers need to reconsider whether plastic is always the enemy but overall live by the mantra of reduce, reuse, repair, and, finally, recycle.

Market-based solutions will struggle, as it is our massive consumption habits which are the root issue and the cheapest solutions will likely not be the best. The Green Alliance noted that there have been calls for more government intervention on plastic waste as well as a more holistic approach to material use.

To truly fix our addiction to plastic we are going to have to avoid the easy answers. Like all aspects of the environmental crisis, the solutions are going to be difficult and require significant change to our way of living but they are out there and becoming increasingly accessible.

14th January 2020

Why is there so much plastic in the ocean?

Plastic pollution in the ocean is a growing problem, but where does it come from? Here are the plastic pollution facts you need to understand what's happening.

You'll likely have heard some stats and facts about plastic pollution in the ocean, like the common warning that there'll be more plastic in the ocean than fish by 2050.

Plastic pollution in the oceans seriously affects sea life – injuring and trapping turtles, dolphins and whales and confusing birds and other creatures into thinking it's food. Ocean plastic therefore very easily enters the food chain, and is consumed by people when they eat fish or shellfish.

But given that it's all man-made, it's not as hard as you think to cut single-use plastic pollution, by aiming to buy better as much as we can – and by putting pressure on those with the power to make changes at scale.

How much plastic is in the ocean and how did it get there?

Researchers have estimated that up to 12 million tonnes of plastic ends up in the ocean every year – that's the equivalent of a rubbish truck every single minute. But how does plastic get into the ocean?

Most of the plastic pollution in the ocean starts out on land. It mainly comes from household and commercial waste, which blows from waste bins and landfill sites into rivers or sewers, then flows out into the sea.

Plastic pollution in the ocean also comes from our clothes. Tiny 'microplastics' escape down the drain when we run synthetic clothing through the washing machine. An average load of laundry might release around 700,000 microplastic fibres, less then a millimetre in length, into the water. These are too small to be filtered and so they end up collecting on riverbeds or washing out to sea.

Around 20% of plastic in the ocean comes from human activities at sea – mostly fishing. In 2019, a Greenpeace report found that each year, 640,000 tonnes of 'ghost gear' – abandoned, lost or discarded fishing equipment – enters the ocean and is left there. That's 50,000 double-decker buses' worth of plastic every year.

How does plastic pollution in the ocean affect sea life? And is ocean plastic harmful to humans?

Plastic in the ocean affects all kinds of sea life. Turtles mistake plastic bags for jellyfish, which they eat, and sea birds often confuse bits of floating plastic with food too – leading to stomachs full of plastic, which can end up killing them.

Whales also eat pieces of plastic. One whale was found washed up dead on a Scottish beach in late 2019 with 100kg of plastic fishing nets and rope, packing straps, carrier bags and plastic cups in its stomach.

And because fishing equipment is designed for actually catching sea life, huge nets and long ropes left discarded in the sea often trap and kill sea creatures. In 2018, around 300 endangered sea turtles were discovered dead, entangled in a ghost fishing net in Mexican waters.

Why do we need to cut single-use plastic as much as possible?

We've seen how broken-down single-use plastics can harm sea creatures. But microplastics also affect human life too. The more plastic that enters the food chain, for example from broken-down single-use packaging, the more microplastics our own bodies are likely to have to deal with too.

Even if you don't eat seafood or fish, there are very real concerns that microplastics in the air and water can have profound impacts on human health. In 2016, researchers found that microplastic particles in food can damage organs and leach dangerous hormone-disrupting chemicals, known to affect immune systems, growth and reproduction.

Can we reduce plastic in the ocean?

Yes – mainly by making sure society makes and uses less plastic in the first place. In 2019, Greenpeace supporters showed how people power works by demanding a reduction in single-use plastic packaging in supermarkets, for example, forcing Sainsbury's to commit to a 50% reduction by 2025.

There's a long way to go, but continuing to eliminate single-use plastic from your purchases – and finding ingenious ways to reuse and refill what you do end up purchasing – is a great place to start.

To avoid contributing to the microplastic pollution from synthetic clothing, choose natural fibres, buy clothes that last, learn how to mend and upcycle, and wash synthetic clothes using a whizzy microplastics guard like the Guppy Bag or Cora Ball.

By cutting out plastics where we can, and pushing the government and plastic-producing businesses to tackle the problem at the source, we can stop plastic pollution from hurting sea creatures and humans alike.

10 June 2020

How Europe's plastic waste exports contribute to ocean plastic pollution elsewhere

What is the link between how we recycle our plastic waste and ocean plastic pollution, and is this simply a reflection of the inequality which exists between the developed and developing world?

By Maxine Vanbommel

The United Kingdom produces a huge amount of plastic packaging waste, with 2.4 million tonnes generated annually, 1.7 million tonnes of which comes from households. This means that the average household produces a minimum of 61 kilograms of plastic packaging waste every single year. The directly available options to process this waste are: landfill, incineration or recycling, or is there another route?

The link between UK plastic waste exports and ocean plastic

Although according to DEFRA the UK's plastic packaging recycling rates reached 46.2% in 2018, well above the EU target of 22.5%, these figures don't provide the full story as a considerable amount of plastic waste is exported for recycling overseas. Data collected only a year earlier by WRAP suggests that in 2017, at least 686 thousand tonnes of plastic waste was exported for recycling, twice the amount recycled domestically.

This practice is not unique to the United Kingdom. A new study by the Ryan Institute at the National University of Ireland, found that almost half (46%) of all post consumer polyethylene plastic waste from European countries was exported outside of its source country in 2017. Yet once this waste crosses the border, it is not always clear what actually happens to it. In fact, the study which analysed UN Comtrade Data suggested that up to 31% of exported plastic waste is not being recycled. They also estimated that between 83,187–180,558 tonnes ended up in the ocean, accounting for 1.3–7.5% of total plastic ocean debris.

What is most remarkable about this new research was that contributions to ocean plastic from exports differed between source countries. For example, the largest flow of ocean plastic came from Germany, while the greatest share all led back to just a few countries, including the United Kingdom. Why is this the case?

Export destinations matter

When it comes to the fate of our exported plastic waste, it is important to consider where it is being exported to. What makes the United Kingdom stand out from other European exporters is that 85% of the main PE plastic exports were destined for non-European countries, such as Indonesia, Vietnam and Malaysia – all of which lack waste management infrastructure. As PhD Researcher George Bishop explains:

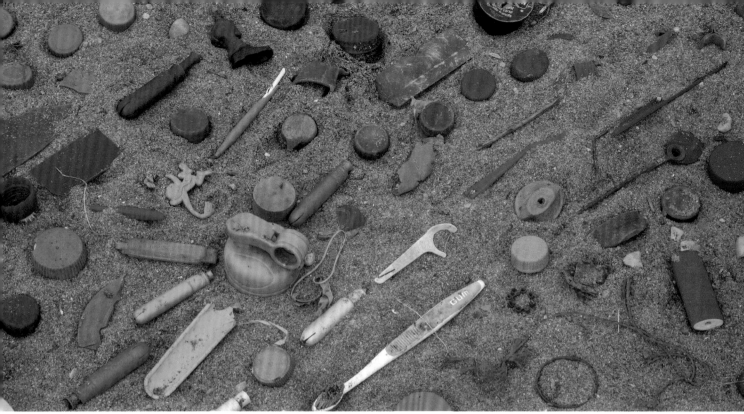

'When countries exported the PE (plastic) outside of the generally high-quality waste management systems of Europe to non-European countries with typically weaker waste management chains, the inadequately managed waste, and thus the PE (plastic) potentially entering the oceans increased.'

While a lack of infrastructure is one thing, further complications arise when plastic waste arriving from abroad is mixed or contaminated and cannot be recycled. We previously reported on the issues surrounding the UKs PRN system, which does not have any checks in place to control the quality of exported material. If not returned to the source country, this waste finds its way to local dump sites or worse.

Last year the Malaysian government said it refused to become a dumping ground, and they vowed to return almost 3,000 tonnes of plastic waste.

'Malaysians like any other developing countries have a right to clean air, clean water, sustainable resources and a clean environment to live in, just like citizens of developed nations.'

Yeo Bee Yin, Malaysia's Environment Minister

Yet this practice of exporting waste continues to happen across Southeast Asia. Figures from Unearthed indicate that the UK government exported more than 300 tonnes of plastic waste per day to non-OECD countries in the first half of this year. While exports to Thailand decreased, countries such as Malaysia saw a rise in 81% compared to last year.

Inequality and ocean plastic pollution

When it comes to ocean plastic pollution, developing countries are often identified as key leakage sources, but rarely does the public narrative address the inequality which sits at the root of this problem. A recent study by the University of Queensland in two remote Indonesian communities illustrated just how precarious the situation is in some of these more remote islands. Plastic literacy tends to be low and the dangers around ocean plastic are not always well understood. Rising living standards coupled with a growing preference for packaged foods over fresh produce due to price and convenience adds to their waste generation. However, without any sort of waste facilities, rubbish is either burnt or disposed of directly into the ocean. These communities are thus faced with not only an environmental catastrophe, but also a progress dilemma.

'The social and economic costs of plastic waste are often borne by those affected rather than those responsible.'

Dr. Anna Phelan

While it is easy to point fingers and shift the problem of ocean plastic elsewhere, socioeconomic inequalities in the developing world, and a lack of quality control in our recycling systems, are a core part of the problem.

By continuing to export our recycling waste abroad to communities which don't always have the know-how nor the facilities to process the waste, is knowingly contributing to ocean plastic pollution. In order to protect our oceans, we should be actively supporting these coastal communities through investments and the development of adequate waste management infrastructure. Yet this should also be extended to what we do at home, to ensure that our recycling systems are up to par.

17 September 2020

www.preventedoceanplastic.com

Why plastics may not always be the worst option for the planet

By Emma Gatten, environment editor

In the struggle to achieve a green life, plastics have become enemy number one. Images of dead dolphins, their stomachs full of plastic bags, and turtles skewered by straws have raised public consciousness of the damage plastics cause in our eco-systems.

But a new report has warned that in the war on plastics, we are at risk of turning to alternatives that could be just as bad, if not worse, for the environment.

Is plastic bad?

Plastic was invented during the Industrial Revolution, and in its early years was seen as a miracle alternative to depleting and expensive natural materials.

It has revolutionised the way we live and is used in everything from medical equipment to make up.

'Plastic is light and durable and has many incredible properties that others don't have,' says Dr Rachael Rothman, the associate director of the Plastics: Redefining Single-Use project at the Grantham Centre for Sustainable Futures.

But the fact it is cheap, hard-wearing and readily available is also what makes it a burden on the environment.

We have come to rely on plastic, using it once and throwing it away. The UK produces 5 million tons of plastic waste every year, with only 26 per cent of it recycled, according to the World Wildlife Fund.

Plastics can take hundreds of years to deplete in nature, where it is detrimental to animal life and ecosystems, and it releases greenhouse gases into the atmosphere if burned.

It's not just a problem of deadly waste: the production of plastic using fossil fuels contributes an estimated 5 per cent of global greenhouse gas emissions which contribute to the warming of the planet.

So should we switch to non-plastic alternatives?

Huge demand, particularly from middle class consumers in the UK's big cities, in the wake of programmes like Blue Planet, has driven supermarkets and other suppliers to seek alternatives to plastic, according to a new report from think tank Green Alliance.

But the alternatives are not always as green as you might think.

Paper bags, which have been adopted by some supermarkets for fresh produce, have a carbon footprint of up to four times that of a single-use plastic bag, and are much more difficult to re-use given how quickly paper tends to fall apart.

A tote bag made from cotton - which requires massive amounts of water to produce - would need to be used 327 times compared to be as carbon efficient as a regular plastic bag, according to a 2008 study. Fine if you only have one, but less good if you've developed a collection.

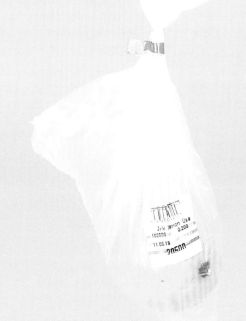

Glass bottles are also significantly more carbon intensive than their plastic alternatives, partly down to their weight - in one study by the Green Alliance a glass bottle was found to use 360g of material, compared to just 10g for a plastic bottle. That adds to its carbon footprint considerably when you take into account the extra transport costs of heavier materials.

Aluminium, which has been hailed as a magic solution to plastic water bottles, has double the carbon footprint of a plastic bottle when it comes to production, though it is also easier to fully recycle.

And while switching to wooden cutlery may feel like the hair-shirt option, it can have a similar impact on marine life if it makes it into the oceans.

What about abandoning plastic altogether?

It's easy to walk around the supermarket and bemoan the amount of seemingly unnecessary packaging on food. But a lot of the time, plastic packaging can prolong the shelf life of food, lowering food waste.

A shrink-wrapped cucumber, for instance, lasts up to six days longer than one with no packaging at all.

Food waste has a huge detrimental cost to the environment, given the often carbon intensive processes that get our food from the ground to our plate, contributing 20 million tonnes of greenhouse gases every year from the UK alone.

What about different kinds of plastic?

Compostable, biodegradable and bio-plastics have all risen in use in recent years as alternatives to traditional plastic. But Green Alliance warns that consumers have become confused by the terms, and don't know how to dispose of them.

'Introducing more types of plastic can be more confusing. And we don't really have a clear national system for recycling,' says Dr Rothman.

Bio-plastics are products made from alternatives to petroleum, often from plants such as corn or sugarcane, but require a huge amount of energy to create - energy that currently comes largely from burning fossil fuels. Meanwhile most of our plastic comes as a by-product of the fossil fuel industry.

Compostable sounds straightforward but in fact very few of these products can simply be thrown on your home compost pile, and instead require industrial composting.

With such an array of products now on the market, it is becoming ever more difficult to work out what can go into your conventional recycling, but including compostable or biodegradable products can often contaminate the entire collection.

So what's the answer?

It's one you know already - reduce, reuse, recycle. Several studies have shown that single-use has the most impact on the environment, no matter what it's made of.

'The problem is the sheer volume we have, it's not the fact it's plastic,' says Dr Rothman. 'It's our throwaway attitude to plastic that is the problem.'

So, if you're concerned about your carbon footprint, keep on using your cotton tote bag. But try not to buy a new one every week.

9 January 2020

Supermarkets putting more plastic on their shelves than ever

Public concern about plastic pollution is at a high, but new research shows that the plastic footprint of the top 10 UK supermarkets has actually increased over the past year. Here's the breakdown.

By Anthony Lewis

The past few years have been a turning point for our oceans. Viral footage of beached whales with plastic in their stomachs, turtles with straws jammed up their noses, and crabs stuck in plastic cups have travelled the world.

We're all waking up to the damage plastic is having on our environment. As a result, a wave of public outrage led to a host of commitments and pledges from supermarkets to reduce plastic.

But how much was actually done? Greenpeace UK and the Environmental Investigation Agency investigated their commitments, and how their promises on plastic measured up to actual achievements.

The results are shocking. Supermarkets now put over 900,000 tonnes of plastic packaging on their shelves a year. Like most plastic, it finds its way into our oceans or goes into landfill.

Last year Greenpeace published its first league table ranking UK supermarkets' plastic footprint. In this year's updated league table there have been some shifts in the ranking, some backtracking, and – more hopefully –some breakthroughs.

Supermarkets are creating a sea of plastic that just keeps getting bigger

The big news is that supermarkets put even more plastic than ever before on their shelves this year. Seven of the 10 supermarkets ranked increased their plastic footprint. All of this at a time when over 1.5 million people have called on them to make dramatic reductions!

There are no real winners or losers in our league table – across the board we are seeing far too much single-use plastic hitting the shelves. This is plastic that customers have overwhelmingly said 'no thanks' to – sometimes literally, by leaving it at the tills.

The bottom performers are yet to embrace refillable and reusable packing at scale and grew their overall plastic footprint from the year before.

The percentage ranking was decided from scores across five categories:

- Promises made on reduction and reuse
- Future plans on reduction and reuse
- Recyclability and recycled content
- Influencing suppliers
- Transparency

Supermarkets plastic policies revealed 2019

overall % score

Morrisons	M&S	Tesco	Lidl	Aldi
51%	43.7%	43%	41.6%	38%

Needs to do better | **Poor**

52%	44%	43.6%	42.3%	39.1%
Waitrose	Sainsburys	co-op	Iceland	Asda

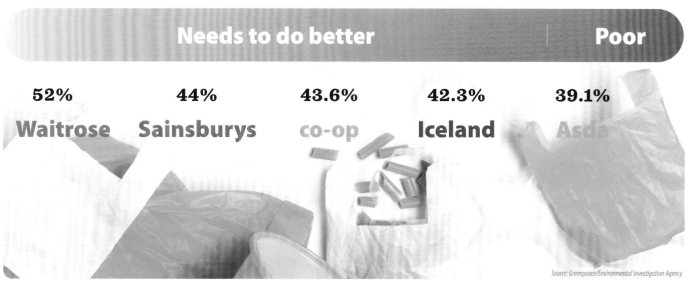

Source: Greenpeace/Environmental Investigation Agency

Sainsbury's were one of the big climbers this year. Having come bottom of the league last year, they now sit more comfortably (but still far from perfect) at third place. Sainsbury's announced plans to reduce plastic by 50%, and introduced reusable produce bags for loose fruit and vegetables. This came as tens of thousands of outraged customers took action against them – the UK's second biggest supermarket business – for their plastic apathy.

Topping the leaderboard this year we have Waitrose and Morrisons – they're there because of their enthusiastic approach toward refillable and reusable packaging. Waitrose also achieved an actual decrease in their plastic footprint this year, along with Tesco and Sainsbury's. Morrisons have also made their loose and refillable ranges cheaper than packaged counterparts.

If refill stations and reusable packaging were introduced in all supermarkets, it would lead to a dramatic reduction in supermarket plastic.

Bags for life are bad for life in our oceans

One area all supermarkets could improve on easily is plastic bags. While the 5p charge may have driven down demand for carrier bags, it's just shifted the problem. Supermarkets sold 1.5 billion 'bags for life' last year – roughly 54 per UK household! That's not a bag for life, that's a bag for a week.

This is a solvable problem. By charging more for bags for life, giving discounts to those who reuse them or bring in their own reusable bags, supermarkets can reduce demand.

Supermarkets also need to be doing much more on throwaway packaging. They pumped out roughly 58 billion pieces of plastic packaging last year. Our oceans mustn't be where they end up.

Shoppers show supermarkets the way

Thanks to ordinary people, speaking up and taking action, there is hope. Whether you're tweeting your supermarket about ridiculous plastic-wrapped bananas, or taking in reusable containers and bags when you shop, supermarkets are taking notice.

Because of you, pumping out pointless plastic is becoming less and less viable for supermarkets. We need to see a refillable revolution hitting the shop floors, and more productive measures to reduce plastic. Thanks to you, supermarkets know what they need to do, now they need to get on with it.

Join over 1.5 million people and tell supermarkets to ditch pointless plastic packaging!

5 December 2019

The above information is reprinted with kind permission from Greenpeace.
© 2021 Greenpeace

www.greenpeace.org.uk

Recycle!

Why is recycling important?

By Ian Barnes

In recent years, climate emergencies have been declared, David Attenborough's Blue Planet II brought home the devastating effects that plastic waste is having on the environment and on wildlife, and there has been an increased emphasis on the need to recycle.

We're a hugely consumer-driven society, and recycling converts the things we throw away into new items, making sure that none of the energy and raw materials used to make them goes to waste. It also prevents the air and ground pollution, and the release of greenhouse gases that results from dumping waste on landfill sites.

But recycling does much more than this. You might think that dutifully putting your plastic bottles and aluminium cans in the recycling doesn't make that much of a difference, but take it from us, it really does.

Why is recycling important?

Recycling preserves precious natural resources

Recycling items rather than using raw materials to make new things preserves the planet's natural resources which, in the face of population growth and growing demand, won't last forever.

It saves energy

Recycling materials uses less energy than extracting, processing, and transporting raw materials to make new products.

It causes far less harm to the environment and animals than extracting raw materials

Think about how raw materials are usually extracted, and what harm these activities might do to the earth. Mining, quarrying, logging, and fracking all cause harm to the planet by causing air and water pollution. These activities can also destroy precious animal habitats.

It reduces the amount of waste that is sent to landfill

Recycling more reduces the amount of waste we send to landfill. When waste sits rotting away on landfill, it leaches toxins into the groundwater and soil, and gives off greenhouse gases like methane as it decomposes, which contributes to global warming. Not only that, if recyclable items are sent to landfill, the precious raw materials and energy that went into making them are lost.

Recycling creates jobs

The more we recycle; the more jobs are created in recycling plants. There will also be more jobs created in recycling innovation and technology, new packaging and product design, and more as the industry develops.

What are the most commonly recycled items?

When it comes to recycling, some items are more widely-recycled than others. These are the materials that are easily recycled and don't reduce in quality once they've been recycled. If you get confused every time you go to your recycling bin, know that these items are no cause for concern.

- Aluminium: This is one of the most easily recycled materials, which is good news, considering how many drinks cans we use. Drinks cans can easily be made into new cans with no loss in the quality of the material.

- Paper and cardboard: Paper and cardboard is usually easily recycled (unless it has excessive tape or embellishment attached or it is soiled). Newspapers in the UK are made exclusively from recycled paper.

- Glass: Glass is easy to recycle and turn into other products like new jars, bottles, and road surfaces. It uses far less energy to recycle glass than to make new glass from raw materials.

What are the hardest things to recycle?

The things that are hard (or virtually impossible) to recycle, are usually items made of a combination of materials. This makes processing very difficult once they reach the recycling plant. Pringles tubes are one of the most obvious examples we can think of when it comes to hard to recycle items. The packaging contains metal, foil, cardboard, and plastic, making it a recycler's nightmare. Other hard to recycle items include:

Black plastic ready-meal and food trays

Black plastic often gets missed by the infra-red sensors used to sort plastic in recycling plants, so it often gets discarded as waste.

Cleaning product bottles

The bottles are often made of a combination of plastics, and if it's a spray bottle, there will be a metal spring in the dispensing mechanism which makes them harder to recycle.

Dental products

Toothpaste tubes and toothbrushes usually aren't accepted for recycling and end up in the bin, though brands like Colgate are taking the lead in introducing initiatives to recycle more dental products.

Clingfilm

It might be handy for wrapping your sandwiches but it's definitely not good for the environment. It's impossible to recycle and can't be reused.

Bubble wrap

Once you pop it, you can't stop, and you usually can't recycle it either. The good news is that it can be easily reused to wrap valuables you're sending in the post or to protect things you have in storage.

Nappies and other sanitary products

There are some brave companies trying to innovate in this area, but generally, these products are a biohazard and can't be recycled.

The netting that wraps your fruit

Those little nets that house your oranges and satsumas so well are unrecyclable and if they are discarded, they can pose a hazard for wildlife who might get trapped in them.

So what about plastics, are they hard to recycle?

When it comes to plastics, recycling gets a little more complicated. PET, the plastic that's used to make water bottles, is widely recyclable, but with other types of plastic, it's not that straightforward.

Know your numbers

If you look at the label on any plastic product, it will have a number from 1-7 on it, inside of a triangle. This is called the plastic resin ID code, which indicates the type of plastic it is and whether it can be recycled or not.

If you see the number 3, 4, or 5 on the label:

If a plastic is labelled 3, it's likely to be vinyl or polyvinyl chloride (PVC) which is used to make food packaging and blister packs for medication.

Type 4 plastic is low-density polyethylene (LDPE), which is used in plastic bags.

Type 5 is polypropylene (PP) which is used to make bottle tops and carpets.

These types of plastics aren't widely recyclable, so the best thing you can do is try to reuse them wherever possible. For example, use plastic bags as bin liners, or to store your child's PE kit or lunch in their school bag, and use bottle tops in art and craft projects.

If you see the number 7 on the label:

Type 7 plastics are known as 'other plastics' and these are usually made from a mix of different plastic resins. Plastics in this group include nylon and plastics like styrene acrylonitrile (SAN), acrylonitrile butadiene styrene (ABS), and polycarbonate (PC). SAN and ABS are food grade plastics, but PC can leach harmful compounds, so if there is a mix of these resins in one product, the chances are, it's headed straight to landfill and can't be recycled.

Our advice is that when it comes to plastics, reduce your use of non-recyclable plastics as much as possible, and reuse any plastic containers that are food safe to store food and snacks.

Does recycling really matter?

This is a question you've probably asked yourself many times. Will it make that much of a difference if you put a few cans, tins, and bottles into your recycling bin every week? The answer is a resounding yes. And if you're still not convinced, here's why.

If you think that recycling your Diet Coke cans is just another pointless chore, think again. Recycling just one aluminium can saves enough energy to power a 100-watt bulb for around 4 hours.

If you think that there's not much point in recycling glass, know that glass can be recycled over and over again with no loss in quality. Add to this the fact that 80% of recycled glass is made into new glass bottles and for every 20 glass bottles you recycle, you save about 2 pounds of carbon emissions, and you'll see how important it is.

These are only a few examples, but generally, the more waste you recycle, the less carbon emissions end up in the atmosphere and this equals a healthier planet, for us, and for generations to come.

What happens if we don't recycle?

The planet might be abundant in natural resources, but at the rate we're using them up, they won't last for long. Then there's the issue of more waste going to landfill, and more greenhouse gases being released into the atmosphere if we don't recycle more. If we don't up our recycling game:

Natural resources and fossil fuels will run out pretty quickly

Current estimates suggest that fossil fuels will run out by 2050. Fossil fuels are used for many things including to make plastics, so if we don't recycle plastics, we have to draw from the precious depleting reserve. Other materials are also running out, from the precious metals used in electronics to the wood from the trees that are rapidly disappearing from some of the world's woodlands and rainforests.

Landfill space will run out

We can't keep producing more and more waste without making an effort to recycle. Landfill space in the UK is running out, and apart from that, sending waste to landfill is an expensive and unsustainable option anyway.

More greenhouse gas will be released into the atmosphere

Greenhouse gases like methane and carbon dioxide contribute to global warming, and the breakdown of the vast mountains of waste on landfill sites is a big contributor. If we don't recycle, this problem will only get worse.

Is upcycling a better alternative to recycling?

Upcycling is becoming ever more popular, and in case you don't quite get what it is, it's taking something that would otherwise be thrown away and giving it a new lease of life. Recycling breaks down an item into its original materials so they can be reused, and upcycling takes an old thing and makes it better than the original. But is upcycling better than recycling?

Upcycling and recycling save waste from landfill and preserve raw materials, but with upcycling, you can get creative with ways to reuse your old items (and you can get the kids involved). Some people even turn a new-found love of upcycling into a money-maker; how many people have you seen selling upcycled furniture and other items that are made from things that probably would have been thrown away?

It's worth remembering though, that not everything can be upcycled, so make good use of your recycling bin in these cases. Otherwise, go and create that shabby chic garden seat from those old wooden pallets in your garage!

How can I recycle more?

Many of us have good intentions when it comes to recycling, but some of us fall short of recycling more whether it's due to confusion about what we can recycle, or the belief that it just takes too much effort.

But here's the thing, recycling more doesn't take a particularly huge effort. Here are some things you can start doing to improve the way you recycle.

Reuse or recycle plastic bags you have

If you have a big bundle of plastic bags at home, either reuse them or take them to a recycling point (many supermarkets have them now). Don't put them in with your recycling bin, as they can clog up the machinery in the recycling plant. Remember your reusable bags when you go to the supermarket so you don't continually add to your plastic bag collection!

Crush plastic bottles and keep the lids on

This removes air from the bottles, creates more space in your recycling bin, and makes recycling more efficient.

Give your recyclables a rinse

Don't put your grease-laden cardboard box into the recycling as it will cause contamination, as will any bottles, jars, or containers that contain the dregs of food or drink. Give them a rinse and you'll avoid contaminating the whole batch of recycling.

Get clued up on local recycling

While confusing, each local authority in the UK has different rules about what it will and won't accept for recycling. Visit your local council's website for information on what you can put in your recycling bin and what has to be taken to a recycling centre or put in with your general waste. With many councils now clamping down on people who flout the rules, it's probably a good idea to get clued up on recycling in your area.

We hope this article has answered some of your burning recycling questions.

Happy Recycling!

24 January 2020

People who are living in the countryside are greener than those in towns, study finds

Nine out of 10 of rural inhabitants recycle their plastic, compared with just seven out of 10 urbanites

By Tom Bawden

People who live in the countryside are considerably greener than city dwellers when it comes to their everyday habits – but much slower to adopt new environmental technologies, a study reveals.

A poll of over 3,000 Brits found a considerable divide between rural and urban areas, with people living in villages and hamlets, on average, adopting more daily green habits than town and city dwellers.

Nine out of ten of rural inhabitants recycle their plastic, compared to just 7 out of ten urbanites, while 56 per cent of them recycle food waste in the country, compared to 44 per cent of those in the city.

Meanwhile, 94 per cent of country livers take their own bags to shops, compared to 81 per cent in the town, according to the poll for the Institution of Engineering and Technology (IET).

More responsible in country

People in the countryside also feel more responsible for protecting the planet, with nearly two thirds believing it's our individual responsibility to address climate change – compared to just half of those living in urban areas.

However, when it comes to green tech, the cosmopolitan cohort takes the reins. Some 45 per cent of urban residents are on green energy tariffs, compared to 30 per cent in rural areas.

Urbanites are also more likely to have installed green technology in their homes.

A greater number of urban respondents have solar panels – 32 per cent versus 9 per cent – battery storage (41 per cent compared to 8 per cent), smart technology (42 per cent against 17 per cent) and heat pumps (36 per cent compared to 6 per cent).

Cities more technologically progressive

'Cities have always been tipped as being more progressive which is demonstrated by the fact that people living in urban areas are more likely to adopt green technologies. However, urbanites are less likely to embrace and put more physical day-to-day green habits into practice,' said IET's James Robottom.

'It's clear that more support and advice is needed to level the balance across all areas and ensure that we are all doing more to play our part in making the planet more sustainable,' he added.

20 November 2020

Recycling rates lower in England's poorest areas

Birmingham and Liverpool among local authorities with lowest rates, analysis shows.

By Tobi Thomas

Recycling rates for household waste are significantly lower in the most deprived areas of England, a Guardian analysis has found.

A breakdown of data from 303 local authorities in England has found that for 2018-19 85% of local authorities that are among the top 20% most deprived have household recycling rates below the overall average of 42%.

By contrast, just one in five of the 20% least deprived areas have a below-average recycling rate.

Deprivation is calculated using the English indices of deprivation, which ranks local authorities from the most deprived to the least deprived. The Department for Environment, Food, and Rural Affairs (Defra) publishes data on household recycling rates, which includes waste sent for reuse, recycling or composting. County councils were not included in the analysis to avoid overlap.

In the borough of Newham in east London, just 16% of household waste falls into this category – the lowest proportion across all local authorities in England.

The local authorities of Birmingham, Liverpool, and Barking and Dagenham are among the 10 local authorities with the lowest rates of household recycling, and are also among the six most deprived local authorities in England.

By contrast, the local authorities of South Oxfordshire, Vale of White Horse, St Albans City and Surrey Heath are among the least deprived local authorities, and all have household recycling rates of more than 60%, putting them in the top six local authorities measured.

Chaitanya Kumar, the head of environment and green transition at the New Economics Foundation, said the relationship between recycling rates and social deprivation was well established, but that the reasons were complex.

He said: 'Access to storage space for waste, high density housing, lack of clear and tailored communication, a more mobile population and the inability to prioritise recycling as a result of poverty are just a few of the structural reasons behind low recycling rates.

'Improving economic wellbeing plus a more focused communications strategy is the way forward to improve recycling rates in underserved communities.'

Cllr David Renard, the environment spokesman for the Local Government Association, said types of housing and whether the local authority was in the city or country had an impact on recycling rates. 'Councils will consider a wide range of factors in determining the most effective type of service,' he said.

'Councils should be free to decide how to deliver their waste services locally and we support the call by the housing,

communities and local government committee for councils to have the flexibility and extra funding to ensure they meet the recycling challenges under the waste strategy.'

A Defra spokesperson said: 'We are committed to ensuring that we go further and faster to reduce, reuse and recycle more of our resources – and our landmark resources and waste strategy will ensure 65% of municipal waste is recycled by 2035.

'We have published guidance to help local authorities boost recycling rates, especially for those who live in flats, and we encourage councils across the country to promote and maintain a consistent recycling service to all their residents.'

Recycling rates have been falling for the past few years despite a longstanding EU target to reach 50% for household waste recycling by 2020, which the UK looks almost certain to have missed.

31 August 2020

Crisps, chocolate and cheese worst offenders for recycling

Which? singles out big brands for lack of environmentally conscious packaging.

By Rebecca Smithers, Consumer affairs correspondent

Crisps, chocolate and cheese are among the worst foods for packaging recyclability, with big brands such as Pringles, KitKat and Babybel singled out for failing to do more to help the environment, a new investigation has claimed.

The consumer group *Which?* analysed 89 of the UK's best-selling branded groceries and found only a third (34%) had packaging that was fully recyclable in household collections. About four in 10 (41%) of items had no relevant labelling, leaving even environmentally conscious consumers in the dark about disposal.

In the exercise, *Which?* looked at 10 different food categories including chocolate, fizzy drinks, crisps, yoghurts, drinks, cheese and bread. Its experts broke down packaging, weighed each element and assessed whether each could be easily recycled.

Their recyclability varied hugely, it found. The worst category by far was crisps, with only 3% of packaging recyclable in household collections. This included Pringles and its notoriously hard-to-recycle tube.

Natalie Hitchins, *Which?* head of home products and services, said: 'Consumers are crying out for brands that take sustainability seriously and products that are easy to recycle, but for any real difference to be made to the environment, manufacturers need to maximise their use of recyclable and recycled materials and ensure products are correctly labelled.

'To reduce the waste to landfill, the government must make labelling mandatory, simple and clear, enabling shoppers to know exactly how to dispose of the packaging on the products they consume.'

Of the chocolate analysed, almost a third of packaging was not recyclable. Nestlé's four-finger KitKats, Cadbury's Bitsa Wispa, Dairy Milk bars and Twirl Bites, along with Mars's M&Ms, were found not to be recyclable in household recycling at all.

From the cheese aisle, snack packs of Cathedral City and Babybel were packaged in plastic net bags, which are not only difficult to recycle but can also get tangled in machinery.

None of the bread packaging *Which?* looked at was recyclable in household collections, although it was recyclable if taken to supermarket collection points alongside plastic bags.

In response to the findings, some manufacturers said that food waste had a larger carbon footprint than plastic waste and claimed that moving away from traditional packaging to recyclable alternatives could lead to compromised, stale or damaged food. Some said their packaging was recyclable at TerraCycle collection points.

Kellogg's, which owns the Pringles brand, said it was 'committed to 100% recyclable, compostable or reusable packaging by the end of 2025', with cans recyclable through TerraCycle points.

Nestlé said it was 'committed to making all its packaging recyclable or reusable by 2025, including the elimination of non-recyclable plastics. We are working hard to get there and have put temporary solutions in place to support recycling in the interim.'

Cathedral City said: 'It is correct that our nets cannot be recycled through kerbside collection. We believe that to be the case for all netted cheese products in the market. We are currently trialling recyclable alternatives to the nets.' Babybel also said it was setting up a UK and Ireland partnership with TerraCycle.

Meanwhile, a new certification scheme is being rolled out by OPRL – the organisation that oversees pack recycling labelling – to bring consistency to claims of recyclability.

Jane Bevis, chair of OPRL, said: 'For some time now we've been concerned about the level of greenwash and over-claiming evident in the packaging market. It's really tough for any but the most practised packaging technologist to keep up with the latest packaging developments such as coatings and colourings and their impact on recyclability.'

24 September 2020

What is zero waste? What is the zero waste movement?

You may have heard the term 'zero waste' or 'zero waste lifestyle' or 'zero waste movement' a lot recently, but what exactly does it mean? What does a zero-waste mean?

Living a zero-waste lifestyle whether at home or in your business, means you strive to use as little single-use plastic as possible, instead opting for sustainable and reusable alternatives. In short, it means you send as little as possible to landfills, which can damage the environment and natural habitat around them. Replacing as much as possible with reusable products includes everything from clothing, to food and drink packaging, to hygiene products, either more sustainable or plastic free, which will ultimately protect the environment, benefit communities and support a circular economy. The 3 R's play an important role in this; Reduce, Reuse, Recycle. This means reducing what you use, reusing as much as you can, send what's left to recycling, and compost what you cannot, then finally the small part of waste left goes to landfill.

Zero waste may sound like an unachievable pie in the sky goal, but it is just a goal, a visionary term with the intention of having a positive impact on the planet. We all know it would be virtually impossible to have absolutely zero waste in our lives. It's not really about perfection; it's about making a conscious effort to make better choices.

What is a circular economy?

While living low waste, reducing, reusing, and repairing as much as we can is wonderful – it's still not circular. The goal of zero waste is to move to a circular economy, which is where rubbish has no existence. The circular economy mimics nature in that there is no garbage in nature. Without a circular economy, we are regularly taking resources from the earth, then sometime after dumping them back in a hole in the ground. Natural resources are so valuable, we can't afford them ever running out! So instead of discarding these resources, creating a circular economy means reusing items or sending them to be recycled, so they can be resumed fully back into the system.

Zero waste means designing and managing products and processes to reduce the volume and toxicity of waste and materials, conserve and recover all resources, and not burn or bury them. Implementing zero waste will help reduce discharges to land, water, or air that may be a threat to planetary, human, animal or plant health, and imitate sustainable natural cycles, where all discarded materials are resources for others to use.

Looking at the big picture, like preventing waste being produced in the first place, is a lot more common now. Many manufacturing companies are looking at designing long-lasting, easily maintainable and repairable products, by reducing packaging and redesigning those products that cannot be safely reused, recycled and composted. By reusing parts and material coming from discarded products, where every 'waste' from one process becomes a source for another such that the utility of the material is maximised, is in line with a circular economy

What's wrong with landfills?

A landfill site, or tip or rubbish dump, is a site for the disposal of waste materials. Waste is

either dumped on the ground, or used to fill a large designated or unwanted hole. The decaying rubbish produces weak acidic chemicals which combine with liquids in the waste to form leachate and landfill gas, which can be toxic.

The U.S. EPA has estimated roughly 42% of all greenhouse gas emissions are caused by the production and use of goods, including food, products and packaging. Reducing, reusing and recycling will conserve that energy and dramatically reduce our carbon emissions. By reducing the amount of trash you create, you could literally save thousands of pounds of trash from entering landfills — proving that one person really can make a difference.

Animals, plants, and future generations are all facing the sad effects of landfill. The food waste found in landfills attracts birds, mammals and rodents alike to feast on leftovers, however it is often not suitable for animals, and can give them food poisoning.

Landfills are changing and destroying animals, natural habitats. Cutting down trees and clearing land to extend our landfill sites is clearing out the homes of hundreds of different species. Loss of habitat is one of the largest threats to 85% of the species in the International Union for the Conservation of Nature (IUCN) Red List, according to WWF.

Not only do landfills have a direct effect on animals, they are having an indirect effect on them too. Waste sent to landfill is often overloaded with chemicals that can disturb plant growth in nearby areas if it leaches into the ground. The chemicals contaminate plants and waters, and as scary as it sounds, this contamination at the very origin of the animal hierarchy means that all species in the food chain could be affected.

Waste in landfills, whether it's biodegradable, plastic, or anything in between, will emit greenhouse gases, which directly contribute to climate change. Read our full blog post here on why landfills cause pollution and are bad for the environment.

Engaging the community

The success of any zero waste goal relies on education and participation of communities and business organisations. Encouraging people to invent & adopt waste free practices and take active participation in the design of the resource management system towards waste reduction would be of

Single use swaps
The rubbish you can save in 1 year!

1x reusable bottle = **167** plastic bottles

1x reusable bag = **170** plastic bags

1x metal straw = **540** plastic straws

1x reusable cup = **500** coffee cups

Source: Unisan

invaluable benefit. Public education campaigns to inspire participation should be carried out, and they need to be well resourced and sustained.

How to start your zero waste lifestyle at home?

There are many simple ways to get started in working towards a zero-waste lifestyle. Many zero wasters recommend beginning by looking through your trash and recycling bins to see what you're throwing out the most.

If your garbage can is filled with food scraps, you could start composting. If your bin is overflowing with paper products like napkins, paper towels, and tissues, invest in some cloth napkins, cleaning cloths (which you can easily upcycle from old towels), and handkerchiefs, or use an eco friendly version. If there is a lot of food packaging, start buying food from bulk sections where you can bring your own reusable container or packaging, or look for foods packaged in recyclable or sustainable packaging.

15 June 2020

25 ways to reduce plastic waste

Is it possible to live a plastic free life? Yes. Is it easy to live a plastic free life? No, I don't think it is, and that's because plastic is in, or comes as packaging on, so many things. However it is achievable to use less plastic and drastically reduce plastic waste in the home.

How to use less plastic

1. Buy loose fruit and vegetables

If you don't have a local greengrocer or farmers market then always choose the plastic free option in the supermarket. Of course don't use the plastic produce bags provided to bag up your loose fruit and vegetables. You can always use the paper bags meant for mushrooms if you haven't taken your own produce bags or buy yourself some reusable produce bags. I just put the fruit and vegetables loose in my trolley and then use a cloth grocery bag at the till.

2. Always carry a cloth shopping bag

Supermarkets do sell 'bags for life' and although they're stronger and last longer than the old plastic bags they're often not recyclable. Get yourself a cloth bag, or make your own out of an old shirt, duvet cover… anything you don't use anymore.

3. Carry a reusable coffee cup

So many disposable coffee cups are thrown away every single day. The lids often can't be recycled and the majority of the cups can't be recycled either because the cardboard is coated in plastic.

4. Use a sustainable lunch box

Great for the kids and will help to stop you buying prepackaged sandwiches and lunches every day during your lunch hour. There are loads of varieties of food containers you can go for, from a sturdy plastic one (go for BPA free) that can be reused or ones made from stainless steel, bamboo, rice husks or even plant based vegan leather which would be even better.

5. Buy tinned soup

I find it very odd that you can buy soup in a bag. So instead of bagged soup or soup in single use plastic containers just make your own or buy tins of soup!

6. Buy meat from a local butchers

Supermarkets often use unrecyclable plastic to display your meat. Butchers don't display their meat in plastic so just take your own containers. Your local butcher is more likely to use locally sourced meat and it's also more likely to be ethically raised as well. Just ask them. Or take your own containers to the meat counter in supermarkets. Better still, reduce the amount of meat you eat as that's better for the planet anyway.

7. Go to a bakery for your bread or make your own

Independent bakeries often still sell bread wrapped in paper, or you can ask them to just put it into your own cloth bag. I've started making my own bread – it's really easy (my first loaf was pretty bad, but they're getting better and better).

8. Bulk buy

Find a zero waste supermarket or shop near you but don't forget to take your own containers so you can fill up on nuts, grains, pulses, oats, rice and dried fruit (as well as much more).

9. Say no to straws

Always refuse straws when in cafes, bars and restaurants and tell the staff why if you're feeling righteous (if enough people tell them they don't want straws, they'll stop buying them). If you really can't go without them buy reusable straws.

10. Never buy bottled water again!

Just buy a reusable water bottle and fill it up at home. Some cafes, bars and restaurants might even fill your water bottle for free. More and more water refill stations are popping up.

11. Stop buying cling film

Use reusable food wraps instead of cling film, they're reusable and biodegradable alternatives to cling film. You can buy beeswax wraps or vegan friendly ones.

12. Buy boxed laundry powder

Buy laundry powder in a cardboard box instead of liquid detergents or better still…

13. Make your own

Making your own laundry detergent, cleaning products, lunches, creams and many other things helps to reduce the

amount of overall waste your house produces. You'll reduce plastic waste quite dramatically by making your own things.

14. Stop chewing gum!

'Chewing gum has been with us since the Stone Age – chicle gum was made from the sap of the Sapodilla tree. Most modern gums are based on a synthetic equivalent, a rubbery material called polyisobutylene that's also used in the manufacture of inner tubes'- Science Focus

15. Swap disposables for reusables

Swap a disposable razor for one where you can just swap the blade instead – check out these safety razors and read why you should buy a safety razor.

16. Choose your takeaways wisely

Only get food deliveries from places that use sustainable packaging or pick up your takeaway yourself and ask them to use the containers you've brought with you. This reduces all kinds of waste (styrofoam, plastic and tinfoil containers). Always refuse plastic cutlery.

17. Buy natural clothing

Most clothes have plastic in them so go for hemp, organic (sustainable) cotton, bamboo or wool (as long as it's ethical). Get out of the habit of fast fashion. You can now even buy eco-friendly underwear (something I struggled to find for ages).

18. Use a handkerchief

Most tissues either come in small packets or boxes with plastic packaging. Using handkerchiefs also reduces your waste.

19. Buy eco-friendly toilet paper

Choose plastic free or recycled toilet paper that comes wrapped in paper – or get yourself a bidet or some reusable wipes!

20. Use lip balm in a tin

Buy lip balm in a tin. I use Trilogy which I bought when I was in New Zealand and it's still going strong 4 years later, just don't use vaseline as it's made from oil, it also might not be as harmless as you thought.

21. Use shampoo bars

Rather than buying shampoo in bottles buy a shampoo bar. They last for absolutely ages and there is no plastic in sight.

22. Ditch the liquid soap

Talking of shampoo bars, replace your liquid soap with a bar of soap as well.

23. Got pets?

Buy tinned food rather than pouches. You can now recycle Lily's Kitchen cat food pouches with Terracycle though. Read how to have an eco-friendly cat.

24. Support local businesses

Many of the smaller local businesses tend to use less plastic anyway, but always try to support the ones who are committed to reducing their plastic packaging, whether that's a shop, leisure facility, restaurant or bar. At the very least support zero waste online shops rather than massive corporations like Amazon.

25. Reuse the plastics you already have

There's no point in just throwing them all away to rid your home of plastic if you can actually make use of something!

Refuse -> Reduce -> Reuse -> Recycle

15 November 2020

7 Ways to reduce waste

We can all make small changes to the way we live. In every moment, we have a choice to make: are you for your world or against it?

We all have a part to play in the recovery of the natural world, but more often than not, it feels like an increasingly impossible task.

The good news is that WWF Ambassador Sir David Attenborough knows where we need to start – by stopping waste in our everyday lives.

'Stop waste. Stop waste of any kind. Stop wasting energy, stop wasting food, stop wasting plastic and stop wasting time. This is a precious world and each of us can use our actions and our voice to save our planet.' - David Attenborough

We can all make small changes to the way we live. In every moment, we have a choice to make: are you for your world or against it?

1. Know what you're wasting

If you're going to start reducing waste in your everyday life, you first need to understand how much you're emitting.

Use our footprint calculator to measure your impact, or download the My Footprint app and find out which simple switches you can make to help save our planet.

2. Stop wasting energy

Good news: we're moving in the right direction. Today the UK has 42% lower emissions than in 1990, mainly due to a rise in renewables, but there's still a long way to go to get to the government's target of net zero by 2050.

Switch to a green energy provider to make sure you're supplied with energy from renewable sources.

Getting a smart meter is a great way to keep on top of the amount of energy you're using. Once you know what you're emitting then you can try and reduce it. Smart meters are part of the solution to decarbonising our electricity grid, and a step towards making Britain's energy greener.

You can reduce your energy usage by using energy-saving lightbulbs, flying less and turning off appliances.

3. Stop wasting food

Food waste is a big problem. One third of food produced for human consumption is lost or wasted. But reducing waste in your household is simple: freeze anything you can't eat while it's fresh; try to buy loose produce so you can select the exact amount that you need; and get creative with what you make from leftover food.

Food production is one of the key drivers of climate change and biodiversity loss. We need to stop wasting food and start eating ingredients that don't destroy precious rainforests and the wildlife that lives there.

4. Stop wasting plastic

By 2050, there could be more plastic in the ocean than fish. We can't let our throwaway culture continue.

Try to swap single use items for sustainable alternatives. Use reusable bags, coffee cups and water bottles.

Everyday items such as clingfilm, teabags and food containers all have zero-waste options too - there are so many ways you can cut down on plastic!

We're working with Sky Ocean Rescue so you can help us protect our oceans by reducing your plastic usage, cutting your emissions and eating sustainable fish.

5. Stop wasting money

One of the ways we are most powerful is with our money – where we spend it and where we don't. There are lots of choices we can make on a day to day basis about buying sustainable and ethical products.

Try to support sustainable, ethical businesses where you can, and put pressure on the companies who are contributing negatively to the environment. Let them know that you care about the future of our planet and want to know what they are doing to change.

Ask your bank or pension provider how they're using your money. Is it invested in sustainable projects? Or contributing to nature's decline?

6. Stop wasting time

In the last 50 years wildlife population sizes have plummeted by an average of 68%. But we know it doesn't have to be this way. With global action to protect wildlife, produce food in better ways, and change what we choose to eat, we can turn things around.

When nature suffers, we all suffer. But we have a prescription, and if we act now we can protect our health and the health of our planet. Take a look at our latest Living Planet Report to find out what action is needed to put nature on the path to recovery by 2030.

Share the *Living Planet Report* with your friends and family and join the fight for your world today. With your help, we can spread the word about how we can create a better future.

7. How Can Businesses Help?

We can all reduce waste in our own lives, but what can businesses do?

Find out the impact your place of work is having on the planet and how it can stop environmentally damaging practices by watching Our Planet: Too Big To Fail and Our Planet: Our Business.

How to cut back on plastic waste

By Daisy Hawker

In today's society, it seems we are suddenly swarmed with news on climate change. Don't get me wrong, it's of course important that people begin to recognise climate change as a threat, but it can also make you feel afraid and helpless. We know the planet is in crisis, so what can we do to save it?

Some seem to think their actions as individuals mean nothing, yet this is far from the truth. When one person stands up and begins to change their lifestyle towards a more hopeful future, they in turn inspire others to make a change, who will go on to inspire more, and eventually everybody will be making important changes for the sake of our future! Even if you are just one person, you can make that difference.

I've been fortunate enough to spend the past year working as a Regional Youth Board member for NCS, where our board's Social Action Project was to help individuals in the South East of England reduce their use of (and recycle) single-use plastics. Single-use plastics are one of the biggest problems our planet faces, with as many as eight billion pieces every day polluting the oceans, contributing to global warming and harming animals. It is vital that we cut down our usage and here are some of my top tips on how to do this:

Make some plastic-free swaps with your everyday items

It's easy to replace items you come across every day with more eco-friendly alternatives – and you'll barely notice! Some personal favourites of mine include: a bamboo cutlery set (super convenient, and hardly takes up any space in your bag), shampoo, conditioner and body wash bars instead of bottles and a menstrual cup over disposable sanitary products. Even better, many plastic-free swaps like this can save you money in the long run!

Cut back on fast/takeaway food

Cue gasps. Yes, I know it sounds hard to give up fast food, but what's more important – a milkshake or your future?! Many restaurants that sell takeaway food use packaging that can't be recycled, and the majority ends up in landfills.

Desperate for a hit of coffee in the morning? Consider investing in a reusable cup. They even sell collapsible cups to keep in your bag for emergencies!

Educate yourself on what can and can't be recycled

Think you know what plastics you can recycle? Check again. It's so important to read up on whether something can be recycled. Some plastics can be recycled at a recycling point, and some may not be safe to recycle in your area. If your area can't recycle much plastic, then make some changes! Get in touch with your local council and raise questions as to why certain things can't be recycled in your area.

Buy a reusable bottle

Okay, sure. You've probably seen this tip a million times, yet so many people still seem to buy and fill up plastic bottles. Not only is this unhygienic, as micro plastics could break down into your water which you will ingest, but when you keep using a single-use plastic bottle over a reusable bottle, you end up throwing it away very quickly due to how dirty it gets.

There are so many reusable bottles of every shape, size and design, so there's no excuse to keep buying plastic bottles. If you're reading this article and you still don't own a reusable bottle, this is your incentive to get out there and buy yourself one now!

Consider plastic-free alternatives in your food shop

It's saddening to see how much plastic supermarkets still use. Although, encouragingly, many are cutting down on things like 5p bags, straws and packaging on fruit and vegetables – but we still have a long way to go.

I'd say I am rather persuasive and I'm pleased to say that my family and I now shop at local markets for fruit and vegetables. Not only do local markets and shops use much less plastic, but you are also supporting a small business. Plus it tastes much better!

These are just some of the changes regarding plastic that you can make. Use the power you have to cultivate a brighter future. Now go out there, canvas bag and reusable bottle in tow, and change the world!

20 July 2019

Key Facts

- The UK is the largest plastic waste producer in Europe and one of the biggest producers of plastic waste in the world. (Page 1)

- 26 million tonnes of general household waste is produced yearly in the UK. (Page 1)

- France is the top country in the world for food sustainability. (Page 2)

- Malta, the world's 43rd richest country, has one of the lowest recycling rates in Europe at just 7%. (Page 4)

- Cigarette butts are littered more than anything else, accounting for 66% of all litter items dropped. (Page 5)

- 30% of people see litter as a problem. (Page 6)

- The most commonly-found type of litter by participants in the Great British Spring Clean 2018 was non-alcoholic drinks-related (77% of participants), followed by alcoholic drinks-related (61%) and fast-food litter (54%). (Page 7)

- During the first lockdown in 2020, 20 million tonnes of annual commercial waste has reduced by about 45 per cent. (Page 11)

- 17 million barrels of oil were used just for producing plastic water bottles in 2006. (Page 12)

- Plastic items can take up to 1,000 years to decompose in landfills. (Page 12)

- If glass is thrown away in landfills, it takes a million years to decompose. (Page 12)

- The UK produced 222.9 million tonnes of waste in 2016. (Page 14)

- There are around 500 landfill sites in the UK. (Page 14)

- The 44 waste incinerators across the UK burned 10.9 million tonnes of rubbish in 2018. (Page 16)

- 12.5 per cent of waste currently goes to landfill. (Page 17)

- Kenya has imposed the toughest plastic bag ban yet, charging up to $38,000 or 4 years in jail for using them. (Page 18)

- The 70% of plastic waste that has been disposed of can be broken down as follows: 79% is either in landfills or in the environment, 12% has been incinerated and 9% has been recycled. (Page 18)

- The world's population of 2.5 billion produced 1.5 million tonnes of plastic in 1950. Today this figure is over 320 million tonnes, and is set to double by 2034. (Page 18)

- One study estimated that it would take 67 ships 1 year to clean up less than 1% of the Great Pacific Garbage Patch. That doesn't even consider the majority of plastic which has sunk to the ocean floors. (Page 18)

- One study found marine plastic pollution in 100% of marine turtles, 59% of whales, 40% of seabirds and 36% of seals examined. (Page 19)

- By 2050, virtually every seabird on the planet will have eaten plastic. (Page 19)

- Nearly one million plastic bottles are sold every minute around the world. (Page 19)

- The average time that a plastic bag is used for is just 12 minutes. And they take up to a thousand years to decompose! (Page 19)

- Plastic production uses around 8% of the world's oil production. (Page 19)

- Up to 12 million tonnes of plastic ends up in the ocean every year. (Page 21)

- An average load of laundry might release around 700,000 microplastic fibres, less then a millimetre in length, into the water. (Page 21)

- The average household produces a minimum of 61 kilograms of plastic packaging waste every single year. (Page 22)

- The UK's plastic packaging recycling rates reached 46.2% in 2018, well above the EU target of 22.5%. (Page 22)

- Supermarkets now put over 900,000 tonnes of plastic packaging on their shelves a year. (Page 26)

- Supermarkets sold 1.5 billion 'bags for life' last year – roughly 54 per UK household! (Page 27)

- Recycling just one aluminium can saves enough energy to power a 100-watt bulb for around 4 hours. (Page 29)

- Current estimates suggest that fossil fuels will run out by 2050. (Page 29)

- Nine out of ten of rural inhabitants recycle their plastic, compared to just 7 out of ten urbanites. (Page 31)

- Out of 89 of the UK's best-selling branded groceries, only a third (34%) had packaging that was fully recyclable in household collections. (Page 33)

- Roughly 42% of all greenhouse gas emissions are caused by the production and use of goods, including food, products and packaging. (Page 35)

- Today the UK has 42% lower emissions than in 1990. (Page 38)

- By 2050, there could be more plastic in the ocean than fish. (Page 38)

Biodegradable waste

Materials that can be completely broken down naturally (e.g. by bacteria) in a reasonable amount of time. This includes organic materials such as food waste, paper waste and manure, which can be composted, as opposed to items such as plastic bottles that would take thousands of years to break down naturally.

Circular economy

Keeping resources for as long as possible in order to extract maximum value from them, and then reusing or recycling the product (or materials from the product) instead of throwing it away.

Conservation

Safeguarding biodiversity; attempting to protect endangered species and their habitats from destruction.

Eco-friendly

Policies, procedures, laws, goods or services that have a minimal or reduced impact on the environment.

Fly-tipping

Sometimes referred to as `sneaky dumping` or `dumping on the fly`, fly-tipping is the illegal dumping of waste in inappropriate areas. People usually do this so they don`t have to pay for bulky items to be collected and removed. Fly-tipping is unsightly and poses a threat to the environment and human health.

Food waste

Around seven million tonnes of food is thrown away by households in the UK every year. Some of the waste is unavoidable, such as peelings or bones, but most of the food is edible. This is because there is often confusion over use-by and best-before dates. Also, many families buy more food than they actually need.

Incineration

A method of disposing of waste by burning it into ashes. Incineration reduces the amount of waste that is sent to a landfill and can even convert waste into energy. However, there are concerns about the environmental impact of incinerators (air pollution, toxic waste, etc.).

Landfill

A type of waste disposal in which solid waste is buried underground, between layers of dirt. Biodegradable products will eventually break down and be absorbed into the soil: however, non-biodegradable products such as plastic carrier bags will not break down (or will do so very, very slowly).

Litter

Rubbish that has been discarded and left lying around rather than disposed of properly. Littering is a crime and people can be fined on-the-spot up to £80.

Microplastics

Extremely small pieces of plastic (5mm or less), which come from plastic pollution in the environment. As plastic is broken down, small fragments break off and can be ingested by sea life, animals and humans. Some microplastics are purposely manufactured for use in cosmetics, such as microbeads. Many companies are phasing out the use of microbeads and replacing them with natural alternatives such as ground almonds or pumice.

Pollution

Toxic substances which are released into the environment: for example, harmful gases or chemicals deposited into the atmosphere or oceans. They can have a severe negative impact on the local environment, and in large quantities, on a global scale.

Recycling

The process of turning waste into a new product. Recycling reduces the consumption of natural resources, saves energy and reduces the amount of waste sent to landfills.

Sustainability

Sustainability means living within the limits of the planet's resources to meet humanity's present-day needs without compromising those of future generations. Sustainable living should maintain a balanced and healthy environment.

The three Rs/Waste hierarchy

The three Rs of recycling are Reduce, Re-use and Recycle. This refers to reducing the amount of waste you make, re-using materials rather them throwing them away (for example, glass milk bottles delivered to your doorstep get used again) and recycling materials by breaking them down and remaking them into something else (plastic drink bottles could be melted down and be made into a plastic chair).

Throwaway/throw-away society

A society where rather than re-using or recycling something, people just throw it away. This is strongly influenced by consumerism, the increased consumption of goods.

Waste

Anything that is no longer of use and thrown away. Each year the UK generates approximately 290 million tonnes of waste, which has a damaging effect on the environment.

Zero waste

A plan to promote the idea of recycling and re-using materials rather than just disposing of them. The aim is to reduce the amount of waste sent to landfills.

Activities

Brainstorming

- In small groups, discuss what you know about waste and recycling.
  - Which countries produce the most waste?
  - How is our waste disposed of (in the UK)?
  - What kind of waste goes to landfill?

- In pairs, create a mind map of all the different types of waste that you can think of.

- In small groups, list different types of waste management (e.g. incineration, landfills, recycling, zero waste, etc.) and create a list of pros and cons. Which method would you recommend?

Research

- Find out which countries are best at dealing with their waste; feed back to your class.

- Find out which countries produce the most waste – how do they deal with it? What policies do they have for reducing waste and increasing recycling?

- Choose a plastic item and do some research into if/how it can be recycled. What type of plastic is it? Is it widely recycled?

- Do some research on your local council's recycling scheme. Compare it to another scheme somewhere else in the UK. Are there any differences? How do they compare?

- Create a questionnaire to find out people's attitudes on litter – do they differ between different age groups or genders?

- Research recycled products. How many different things are made from waste? Can you think of anything that can be made from waste?

Design

- Choose one of the articles from this book and create an illustration that highlights the key themes of the piece.

- Design a poster that illustrates the litter statistics from the article 'Litter and littering in England 2017 to 2018'.

- Design a storyboard for a Youtube video which will encourage people to reduce their plastic waste. You could plan to use actors or animations. Include some information about why it is important for plastic waste to be reduced and some tips on how to do so.

- Design a leaflet that will be distributed by your local council to draw attention to the negative effects of fly-tipping.

- Create a poster to promote recycling in your school.

- Using the article '31 Facts you wish you didn't know about plastic waste', create a poster to display 10 of the facts.

- Design a poster to promote litter-picking. What things can you include to persuade people to collect litter in their area?

- Choose an item of rubbish that you have at home that can be up-cycled. You could use a jam-jar to make a vase, or a tin as a pencil holder. Use your imagination and make sure the item is safe and clean before starting.

Oral

- In small groups, discuss the pros and cons of incineration and landfills.

- Do we have a moral duty to recycle our rubbish? Discuss this question as a class.

- In small groups, discuss ways that we can reduce single use drinks containers. List some ideas for alternatives.

- In pairs, discuss ways that you can reduce the amount of waste you produce at home. How many things can be reused or recycled?

Reading/writing

- Write a letter to the organisers of a music festival in your local area, explaining why it is important they try to minimise waste at the festival and suggesting ways in which they might do this.

- Write a report on the use of microplastics in cosmetics for your school or local newspaper. Use the articles in this book and online research, and write at least 500 words.

- Write a list of items that you or your family have thrown away in the last couple of months. Try to think of some alternative uses for these things. For example, that old t-shirt you threw away could have been re-used and turned into a pillowcase.

- Watch a documentary on waste or recycling. Write down things that you didn't know before watching – will you change your behaviours now?

- Write a persuasive letter to your local MP to help improve recycling facilities in your area.

- Write a letter to a supermarket to persuade them to use less plastic in their packaging.

Acknowledgements

The publisher is grateful for permission to reproduce the material in this book. While every care has been taken to trace and acknowledge copyright, the publisher tenders its apology for any accidental infringement or where copyright has proved untraceable. The publisher would be pleased to come to a suitable arrangement in any such case with the rightful owner.

The material reproduced in *ISSUES* books is provided as an educational resource only. The views, opinions and information contained within reprinted material in *ISSUES* books do not necessarily represent those of Independence Educational Publishers and its employees.

Images

Cover image courtesy of iStock. All other images courtesy of Pixabay and Unsplash, except pages 19: Freepik.

Icons

Icons on pages 6 & 12 were made by Freepik from www.flaticon.com.

Illustrations

Simon Kneebone: pages 10, 22 & 34.

Angelo Madrid: pages 2, 25 & 30.

Additional acknowledgements

With thanks to the Independence team: Shelley Baldry, Danielle Lobban, Jackie Staines and Jan Sunderland.

Tracy Biram

Cambridge, January 2021